ABRAR ANSARI

Management by
INTENT

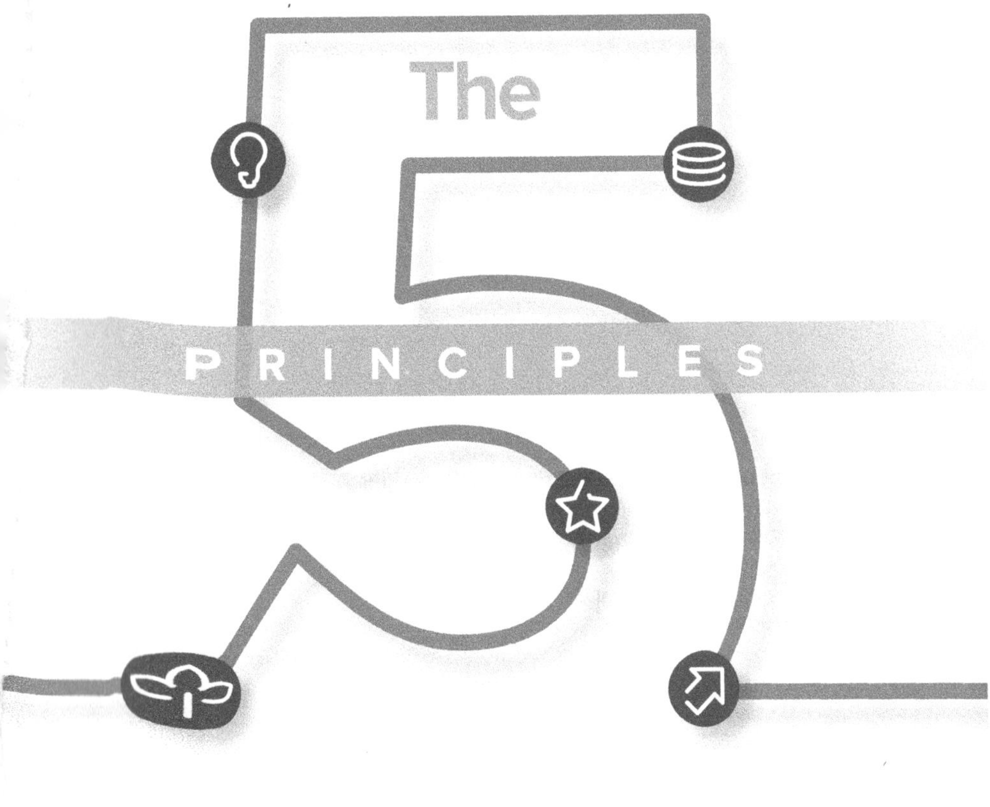

The 5 PRINCIPLES

Management by Intent, the Five Principles Copyright © 2020 by Abrar Ansari
All rights reserved. Printed in the United State of America.
No parts of this book may be used or reproduced in any manner whatsoever without written permission except in the case of brief quotations embodied in critical articles or reviews.

Requests for permission should be addressed to: **info@abstract-space.com**
For mor information, please visit: **ManagementbyIntent.com**

ISBN: 978-1-7357678-0-2
Library of Congress Control Number: 2020917738

Design and production: Sergio Analco

I dedicate this book to all those who coach and mentor others. People who shape intellects, mold characters, and uplift our spirits; stewards of knowledge who selflessly impart their wisdom to all who seek it, without judgment or agenda. These are the people I have looked up to all my life. Without them as guideposts and beacons, none of us would be on a path to personal growth and fulfillment.

Contents

Acknowledgments	VII
Preface	IX
CHAPTER 1. The Legacy That Shaped Me	1
CHAPTER 2. Realigning Our Sense of Purpose	9
CHAPTER 3. The Knowledge of Self	19
CHAPTER 4. Retrofitting the System	25
CHAPTER 5. The Principle of Preservation of Life	31
CHAPTER 6. The Principle of Preservation of Dignity	37
CHAPTER 7. The Principle of Preservation of Reason	43
CHAPTER 8. The Principle of Preservation of Wealth	49
CHAPTER 9. The Principle of Preservation of the Future	57
CHAPTER 10. Management by Intent	65
Notes	73

Acknowledgments

MBI has been 20 plus years in the making. I have always dreamed about this day, but was never sure if it would become a reality. It has been a burning desire of mine, since my college days, to put something like this together. The roads I have traveled to get to this point are many. All seemed now, predestined to connect me with the right personalities, nudging me, encouraging me, cajoling me to express my thoughts and my ideas along the way. Each step I took, seemingly futile at times, brought me closer to the realization of this dream; a hope to ink something worthwhile and impactful that will allow me to leave a legacy behind.

This journey would not have been possible without my parents' love and guidance. It would have been incomplete without my siblings, meaningless without the companionship of my wife, and void of color without my colleagues.

I would like to say a special thank you to the following individuals for their support:

- Vaseem Ansari
- Nejia Ansari
- Judy Analco
- Asad Faruqi
- Sama Faruqi
- Johnathan Iheanacho
- Kate Sellers
- Marianne Brown
- Ramana Kullori
- Elise Krentzel

Preface

The Quest for Purposeful Outcomes

AS A MANAGEMENT consultant for 28 years, I have had the privilege of working with global clients in the energy, chemical, pharma, utility, and manufacturing sectors. Whether it was change management, strategy development, coaching, or technology deployment, the experience provided me with opportunities to witness firsthand how organizational values impact leadership behaviors and shape corporate culture.

Over the years, I have argued that business growth strategies based on holistic operational frameworks create more purposeful outcomes that go beyond financials to take into consideration the impact on stakeholders not currently valued. For example, when building pipelines or extracting natural resources, do companies respect the rights of indigenous people and treat them as equal partners in evaluating adverse environmental, economic, social, cultural or spiritual impacts on their lands or resources? Or when implementing employee safety campaigns, instead of invoking fear-based tactics to make employees comply, do employers utilize logic, data, and common sense to genuinely communicate the rationality for safeguarding life to their employees?

These questions piqued my curiosity and disturbed me simultaneously. Having worked closely with a diverse portfolio of clients over the years, from mega global entities to small non-profit start-ups, I have had hands-on experience with all levels of management, including senior executives and facility-level operational teams. Regardless of the level of maturity, size or sophistication, organizational intent predominantly focuses on revenue growth, earnings through cost-effectiveness, retained earnings, and dividends. Consequently, the result is more of the same (i.e. a myopic focus on profitability at all expense).

Boeing, for example, with a single-minded focus on maintaining market share, overlooked its long tradition of adherence to engineering excellence. In their push to gain a larger global market share, Volkswagen committed blatant fraud by falsifying emissions data. Boeing's negligence resulted in the loss of life. Volkswagen's deception impacted air quality, further exacerbating the climate crisis, putting the future health of our planet at risk.

These two examples show that growth, when solely based on financial gains, is a skewed approach to understanding the interconnected global reality of the 21st century. Such exploitations, whether the extraction of natural resources, underpaying workers, or polluting the environment, are all examples of 'business as usual', where the ends justify the means.

Yet there is hope. In the last decade, society has undergone a major shift. Globally, people have started to renounce capitalism's acute allegiance to shareholders. Businesses are waking up to the fact that our survival as a species consists of other factors besides financial profit. Whether it is investing responsibly, signing on to climate change accords, triple bottom line accounting practices, or moves toward a more equitable and compassionate form of capitalism, the shift has begun. It demands recognition and inclusion of often-overlooked stakeholders—the workforce, surrounding communities, natural resources, other species—and their intricate relation to the corporate organism.

This trend towards a more holistic and balanced approach to growth requires a higher level of leadership and consciousness. High-performance leaders of today cannot use the same playbooks to chart a course for tomorrow. The enormity of the challenges we face require revolutionary thinking, one that infuses purpose back into the equation, with the intent to transform the way we run our businesses.

I believe now is the time to introduce what I have coined **MANAGEMENT BY INTENT (MBI)**. **MBI**'s early adapters are organizations that recognize a more profound sense of purpose and want to transform accidental practices into intentional ones. In this book, I break down how management can systematically reach a higher level of consciousness to attain this mission.

My **MBI** journey would probably not have started, had it not been for divine intervention, which I believe in firmly. I now see that everything happens for a reason. During my sophomore year in college, I was late to register for the semester. A senior-level systems philosophy course was the only one available that could fulfill my elective requirements. Begrudgingly, I signed up for it. In hindsight, it was a blessing in disguise.

Since graduating from college, I spent countless hours researching, consulting, reading, exploring, listening, and contemplating how universal ethical principles can impact business decisions to bring about the ultimate balance between thought and action.

This book is the culmination of three decades of introspection—part study, part practice—to bring to life conscious intent, resulting in purposeful outcomes. **MBI** is a call for action to transform and recalibrate corporate culture through:

1. A more accountable and transparent governance framework.
2. An operational structure that is purpose-driven.

My research suggests that purposeful outcomes are achievable through the application of five critical principles: preservation of **life, reason, dignity, wealth**, and the **future**.

Before any transformation of governance and operational frameworks can take place, knowledge of self is the critical first step in undertaking the **MBI** journey. This reflective process is governed by what I call the Al-Ghazali model, which explains how to achieve a balanced organizational psyche, and provides a method to create harmony between the cognitive, emotional, and behavioral dimensions of the mind.

Armed with knowledge of the self and the five preservation principles, leaders will be able to balance the organizational psyche, injecting purpose back into the fabric of the business. We see some early indicators of organizations which are correcting course, taking baby steps in promoting and instituting environmental, social, and corporate governance reforms. Others are stepping up to the plate to address the many consequences of myopic capitalistic growth strategies. **MBI** provides an inside-out perspective and solution to aid high-performance leaders facing challenges in rewriting the wrongs of a free enterprise system gone sideways in the past 50 years.

Chapter 1
The Legacy That Shaped Me

> The beginning is the manifestation of the end.
>
> — ibn 'Atā Allāh,
> 13th century Egyptian Sufi Jurist

LOOKING BACK AT the 30-plus years of my conscious and, at times, unconscious struggles of attempting to keep the material and spiritual aspects of life in balance, I cannot help but appreciate the many people that influenced me over the years. It is to them I owe my current value system, steeped in a long lineage of Sufism, that can be traced back to Mecca, which provides the fundamental building blocks of my approach towards business and life.

Sufism is one of the mystical schools of practice in Islam. It leans towards humanity's inward spiritual development, rather than the outward material aspects of the human experience. Over 1,400 years old, many of its tenets are today considered New Age. Sufism has produced some of the world's most profoundly contemplative literature, such as the poetry of the 13th-century Persian theologian, Jalāl ad-Dīn Rumi.

Both my maternal and paternal grandparents were first-generation immigrants to Pakistan from India. In 1947, when the British departed from the Indian subcontinent, they left behind a cruel legacy of division; historians estimate some 14 million people were displaced by the partition of India and Pakistan, while more than two million were killed. It was one of the bloodiest divides in modern history. Although well settled in India for generations, the way my grandparents handled their migration to Pakistan was with spiritual consciousness. India had, for millennia, embraced multiple faiths. Yet the brutal partition of the country changed that. My father told me the story of how his parents were offered leftover estates in Pakistan, previously owned by a Hindu businessman, who had fled to India. My grandparents felt it was not right to take over someone else's property, and therefore refused to claim it, unlike many other migrants. Those who took that advantage became instantly wealthy. On the other hand, my family traded a life of material comfort and headed to Pakistan, where they felt they would be able to practice their religion freely. At the time, the situation in India was violent and unstable.

After safely bringing my grandmother and family over to Pakistan, my maternal grandfather went back to India, as he had unfinished obligations to fulfill. He knew full well that he might not be able to make it back, but he was an honorable man who lived an ethical life. His commitment to fulfilling his obligations was a central part of his spiritual upbringing and practice. He could not turn his back on what his moral compass dictated, despite the danger. My mother never saw her father again after that trip.

My grandparents were principled people, with a high moral compass. The challenges they faced and the sacrifices they made gave them a solid sense of meaning. They knew that life was worth living, and what standing one's ground really meant. I was fortunate to have them gracefully pass on this knowledge to me in the hopes that I, too, would pay it forward to other generations. My belief system is a product of that grounding which, to this day, fortifies my values and shapes my personality. Similarly, the cultural and religious upbringing of so many others shape who they are today.

I remember being counseled by my maternal great grandmother, when I was very young, to do the right thing. At the time, she was over 90-years-old and blind, yet still mentally sharp and physically active. My mother continues to repeat a specific incident to this day: Summoned to my great grandmother's room (it is common for families and multiple generations to reside together), she asked me if I had mixed water in her body oil canister. She used to leave the container outside in the sun every morning as part of her beauty treatment. For a young boy, pouring water into that container seemed very logical in a scientific experimental kind of way, besides being a fun thing to do. Standing next to her bed with my hand in hers, she questioned me in a calm yet stern voice.

I could not lie to her and admitted my guilt; I poured water into the container to see what would happen when the two elements mixed. Expecting to get punished for my mischievous deed, she instead told me that she would not punish me because of my honesty. From that day on, I was wired to not lie. My great grandmother showed me two things: mercy was more powerfu than justice, and honesty builds trust.

I continued to question the relationship between intent and actions resulting from intentional behavior. I noticed that it required self-reflection, and that was what kept our value system activated. Some call this self-reflection 'meditation' or 'deep thinking'. Whatever the label, it creates a sense of consciousness, connecting us to our virtuous self, that part within us that knows right from wrong.

That consciousness facilitates the opening up of a portal, allowing us a glimpse into our psyche. Once the door is flung open, it is nearly impossible to shut. This type of inward journey can produce an even higher level of consciousness, if and when our psyche is behaviorally, emotionally, and cognitively balanced.

Those with balanced psyches tend to have the following admirable tendencies:

- Courage to stand up and admit their mistakes.

- The ability to show mercy when wronged.

- The wisdom to do the right thing, even when it is against self-interest.

- The resolve to align their intentions with their actions.

Besides growing up in a home steeped in mysticism, my extended family was artistically inclined. My paternal grandfather was a poet, as am I. Poetry had a profound effect on my future systems thinking capabilities. As a youngster, my mother noticed how I struggled with Urdu poetry, so she asked her cousin to tutor me. Although I had trouble with it, I was lucky to study under his tutelage. Over a period of two years, her cousin would show up at our doorstep, despite my unwillingness to participate. I had to comply with his wishes for a couple of reasons. First, respecting one's elders was a cardinal rule. Second, I could not, in good faith, allow him to just show up for no purpose. Ghosting was not an option.

He took a standardized approach to poetry analysis by taking a few verses to dissect meaning. My job was to transcribe. One day, he got lost in dictation, and as my hand was becoming numb from transposing the copious flow of his thoughts on paper, I questioned the validity of his analysis as it was contrary to what I had learned in school.

I wondered how the same set of words could invoke such different meanings. He told me that a good poem uses metaphors and similes to represent symbols and meanings, transcending time and space. A good poet can invoke critical thinking on multiple levels, but the ability to think critically does not mean one can think of all possible meanings.

I later learned that very same concept in systems philosophy. It is called multifinality; that is, the same system's elements can give multiple outcomes, depending upon the way the system is leveraged. A thoughtful reading of a poem requires an understanding of the dynamics between the metaphors and similes, and the meanings depend on the lens we apply. The mindset we bring to decipher the words informs what we see as the interrelationship between the words, tone, acuteness or abstractness of the interwoven ideas that the poet plays with to invoke emotion in the audience.

Before arriving in the US, at the age of 18, the seeds of inward reflection and the systematic deconstruction of ideas were well planted and sown. Yet the nourishment needed for them to take root and sprout was missing until my education started.

There seemed to be an endless array of options at the University of Maryland, where I went to school, just like there were in the supermarkets. It made my head dizzy. The list of degrees one could pursue seemed endless. In Pakistan, there were only a handful of choices: medicine, engineering, or business administration. During that first semester, I barely made it through the coursework. Not happy with my grades or indecisiveness, my counselor advised me to take a career assessment test. Based on the results, my top-tier choices were either fire protection engineering or industrial technology.

I remember meeting with the dean of the fire protection engineering school first. I was not impressed with his pitch. The fact that I would have to take four semesters of calculus was a significant barrier in pursuing a degree in fire protection engineering. I then went to meet with the dean of the industrial technology department. As a seasoned career professional, he had taken on this new role after retiring from the industry.

He was a much better salesperson. I was fascinated with the way he pitched the program to me. Industrial technology offered me the flexibility to explore my intellectual desires, besides providing me with a guided roadmap to follow. That got me excited.

During my third semester, in my systems philosophy class, I learned about biologist Ludwig von Bertalanffy's general systems theory. Little did I know that the study of systems philosophy would redirect my intellectual curiosity on a fascinating inward voyage; one where my mind and belief system would come together seamlessly. A pilgrimage that would, for the first time, lead me to understand the symbiotic relationship between thought and action.

Bertalanffy observed that everything in nature is composed of systems that are both systems in themselves (wholes), or subsystems (parts) of other networks. An excellent example of this is the atom. Two atoms of hydrogen combine with one of oxygen to form a molecule of water. As we know, water is the essence of life on earth. Similarly, like atoms, people come together to build businesses. Collectively, businesses create a free market system, which fuels trade and commerce on a global scale, and is thereby a critical component of the world economic system.

Unlike man-made systems, natural systems are optimized for efficiency and are intrinsically balanced. You would not find three hydrogen atoms trying to link up with two oxygen atoms to create a different type of water molecule. You also will not find water in the natural system being wasted. The water cycle is balanced: evaporated water comes down as rain and is recycled into the soil. So, what is it that makes man-made systems inefficient and wasteful?

The class had lengthy discussions on the theory of reasoned action, behavioral intent, and the role of rationality. Through understanding the dynamics of its parts, we learned how to predict the characteristics of the whole system. We learned how Aristotle's expression—'the whole is greater than the sum of its parts'—forms the basis of systems thinking.

The summer after my graduation, I found an internship with a subsidiary of a global pharmaceutical giant. This North American branch was a chemical lab specializing in the analysis of organic and inorganic compounds. The company had 18 positions open for interns, and hired me to work in the field services department as an industrial hygiene technician.

These technicians were tasked with monitoring the removal of hazardous materials during construction and renovation, demolition, and decontamination. Some of the dangerous materials we had to work with included asbestos, lead, Polychlorinated Biphenyls (PCBs), and other heavy metals. The district manager informed me that only two of the 18 interns would make it to full-time positions after the summer. It was clear to me that to get one of those coveted positions, I had to give it all I had, and more!

On the very first day of my field monitoring assignment, I got stuck in traffic. I did not reach the office until after the team had left for their field assignment. The district manager, known for her iron fist management style, called me into her office and gave me the third degree. By the time she finished, I was literally in tears. As a punitive measure, I was pulled off the field assignment and made to do clerical activities.

Demoted even before I started, I felt rejected. For the next two weeks, as the field teams returned to the office, I was tasked with photocopying and filing their paperwork. Each technician had up to five different types of forms, along with their daily field logs, and each package would typically have about 20 pages. With 17 interns and 20 full-time field consultants, I had to collate and file about 740 pages daily. It took me about a week to get to learn the ins and outs of the document filing process.

Being stuck in the office, however, turned out to be a blessing in disguise. It led me to pick up on the inner workings of the company: the office politics, management style, power dynamics, and the relationship challenges between management and field employees.

When I finally got sent back to the field, because all the other interns were assigned other projects, they made me the designated floater. As a result of floating from project to project, I received the most diversified internship experience and exposure that the others did not.

I met senior consultants and got an earful from them about their problems with scheduling and overtime, forced weekend work, scarcity of field equipment, and pay and bonus issues. I also gained valuable experience and learned about the clients' working styles, needs, and contractual preferences. While I adapted to the daily grind of fieldwork, my systems thinking mindset kicked in. I started noticing the patterns, relationships, and causal loops between different elements within the organization.

I slowly began synthesizing the various processes I witnessed to find better ways of managing the complaints I heard from senior consultants. Before the end of the internship, I presented my plan to the district manager: a color-coded document management system, with templates for reporting and my analysis to improve relationships with the field consultants. At the end of the Summer, not only was I given the full-time position, they promoted me to Field Services Supervisor. I was only 23-years-old.

In retrospect, had I not been late, I would not have learned about the company's system of governance and operations. That gave me the ability to see the multiple moving parts of the organization's policies, and to comprehend how each department fits into the larger purpose of the company.

It did not take me long to realize that the ideas I put to paper did not transform the organization as I had envisioned, even though these ideas reduced costs, saved time, and improved the quality of fieldwork.

There was minimal trust between the field staff and management who were myopically focused on short-term profitability. Monthly financial targets superseded everything else. Items that were off the docket included pay increases, bonuses, and equipment purchases. Because of management's single-minded focus on financials, in retaliation, the staff regularly cut corners, fudged their expenses and timesheets, and hoarded sound equipment.

During my first year as a field supervisor, I was not only responsible for my team's well-being in the field, but was also supposed to champion their cause in all areas of administration. I advocated for issues like overtime pay, raises, and bonuses. It dawned on me that management was not necessarily made up of 'bad people'. Some of them had risen from field positions themselves. It was as if, individually, their intentions were good, but their collective organizational actions were misaligned.

The system had lost its focus on preserving the dignity of its people. Not being able to change direction, the company did what most companies frequently do to improve performance; they reorganized. As a result, 80% of the field staff, including myself, were let go. The explanation given to us was that the parent company did not think field services were in line with their core business objectives. Later on, I found out that they scaled up their field services when their business picked back up.

Stressed as I was for not having a job, I could not stop thinking about the disconnect between performance imperatives and practical realities. My quest for mapping my value system to the systems thinking paradigm now turned into a quest to decipher a systems approach for realigning organizational purpose to organizational intent. The field services concept by no means was out of alignment with the core business of the company. Rather, it served as a tactical advantage, complementing their strategic growth. But since management took the easy way out to cover and short-circuit underperforming financials, they cut staff to improve the bottomline.

My next job leaned more towards the field of management consulting. I joined a small firm that had a unique proposition where I could cut my teeth: management consulting and information technology. I became part of a team that was managing contracts with the International Monetary Fund (IMF) and the World Bank.

It was not too long after that I began reporting directly to the CEO of the firm. I took over the consulting division. As part of my portfolio of accounts, I inherited all IMF and World Bank projects. My quest to decipher a systems approach for realigning organizational purpose to organizational intent took a new turn. I found myself walking the halls of these two veritable organizations, rubbing shoulders with highly intellectual and gifted bureaucrats from all over the world: diplomats, global program directors, and policymakers.

I discovered both these institutes offered congregational prayer services on Fridays to staffers, global dignitaries, and diplomats of the Islamic faith. Attendees were both professional and intellectual. The subjects of the short sermons and lectures given before prayers, by resident and visiting dignitaries, were predominantly focused on enterprise management. Topics included organizational management, stakeholder engagement, labor relations, economic reform, social justice, systemic reform, and social equity. If I found myself in the vicinity on Fridays, I would attend prayers there.

Having been exposed to the Judeo-Christian culture growing up, I understood the topics presented were fundamental to maintaining justice and balance in society: equity, integrity, and fairness. I could map how these were found in many religious teachings and, therefore, were universally accepted.

I discovered the underpinning of the systems model that I was beginning to build was faith-based, yet universal. It rested upon universal values dealing with social justice, commerce, leadership, human development psychology, and organizational management. It just happened that my personal lens was faith-based. My ability to connect the dots has led me to organize a set of universal principles into a comprehensive framework through which to govern businesses for holistic outcomes. My framework addresses the balance required to maintain equity, integrity, and fairness when making business decisions, and to also balance the businesses' responsibilities towards all stakeholders, not just shareholders. I have named the framework: **MANAGEMENT BY INTENT (MBI)**.

This book outlines the construct of **MBI**. I believe this framework leverages universal credo and values to provide a roadmap for realigning the organizational psyche. **MBI**'s purpose is to uncover and, in some cases, discover an understanding of the balance corporations need to strike to serve the public interest for the greater good of society.

It is my belief and experience that if an organization's decision-making bodies adopt the **MBI** framework, its business outlook will be transformed from one of shareholder-servitude to stakeholder-consciousness. As a result of implementing an **MBI** framework, the corporate strategy will no longer be focused exclusively on financial profitability, but expand to include equity and fairness for all stakeholders (i.e. employees, vendors, suppliers, customers, local communities, and shareholders).

When the unconscious psyche, conscious thoughts, and intentful behaviors of organizational minds are aligned towards a more stakeholder-centric sense of purpose, decision-making naturally becomes more holistic. Within the **MBI** framework, I refer to this level of alignment as 'purposeful thinking'. With this purposeful thinking, we can begin to deconstruct the cause and effect of our intentions and resulting practices from a balanced perspective to determine the impact of organizational decisions.

The best outcome for an organization that follows the **MBI Framework** is to not only create value in society through goods and services, but to also uphold the trust given to it by all stakeholders. The **MBI Framework** rest on five foundational principles, which are:

 **Life** is safeguarded

 **Dignity** is preserved

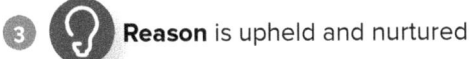 **Reason** is upheld and nurtured

 **Wealth** is protected

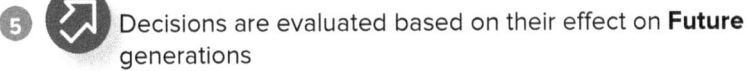 Decisions are evaluated based on their effect on **Future** generations

This book will outline and explain the foundational aspects of the **MBI** philosophy and its underpinning framework. I encourage all thought leaders to explore and leverage **MBI** to enact the transformational changes needed to ensure sustainable long-term growth for their organizations, employees, stakeholders, and the world at large.

Chapter 2

Realigning Our Sense of Purpose

> The purpose of business is to produce profitable solutions to the problems of people and the planet, and in the process it produces profits.
>
> — Colin Mayer,
> Professor of Management Studies at Oxford University

MY PERSONAL QUEST has been focused on gaining a clear understanding of what constitutes balanced and equitable corporate governance and operational frameworks. I have dedicated my career to researching integrated methodologies for improving process excellence, such as Six Sigma, International Organization of Standards (ISO), Baldrige, and others. Yet they all fall somewhat short in linking the *why* with the *what*. With **MBI**, I have added a more philosophical underpinning for organizational management to chart a course towards a more holistic and sustainable management approach.

In his 2019 lecture at Oxford, Professor Colin Mayer spoke about the need to reconceptualize the business model of the 21st century. He said that businesses could not profit from producing problems for the people and the planet. Instead, they should be committed to their purpose and to those who helped them get to where they are. That, in turn, creates 'reciprocal relationships', which engages the employees, makes suppliers more reliable, shareholders and communities more supportive, and customers more loyal. The mutual inclusiveness creates a level of trust that bonds the stakeholders together (i.e. we are in it together, solving problems for the people and the planet).

Most businesses initially think of this concept as resource-intensive and cost-heavy, which cuts into their shareholder profits. Profit is their sole endgame, but are they aware of the negative impact on their other stakeholders, their communities, and the environment? These negative impacts can no longer be ignored and are being questioned by the employees, customers, suppliers, and communities. When the financial gains are measured against the negative impact, what is the bottom line?

Businesses are failing to realize that a more engaged and accountable approach eventually returns greater revenues, and extends the life of the business by gaining social trust.

We see a glimpse of that reciprocity by some organizations amidst the COVID-19 pandemic. When the activewear retailer Lululemon closed its stores in North America and Europe, from March 16 through March 27, it continued to pay its workers for their hours during this time. The brand's workers also received pay for 14 days if they were asked to self-quarantine. Microsoft announced it would pay its hourly workers regular wages, even if they work shortened hours. They also pitched in $1 million to the Seattle Foundation for the COVID-19 Respond Fund. Likewise, it is encouraging to see Amazon, Expedia, Facebook, Google, and Salesforce announce similar initiatives. But why does it take a catastrophic event to get a business to realize their employees are valuable stakeholders whom they need to take care of? The answer is that company officers trade in the long-term purpose of the enterprise for short-term gains.

I firmly believe that the 'short-term' mindset can be recalibrated to focus on long-term goals and objectives fueled by reciprocity and mutual respect for all stakeholders. It starts with realigning our intentions to a two-part commitment:

1. Preventing that which is harmful.

2. Promoting that which is good.

Our intentions are a manifestation of our value systems, experiences, and commitments. In **MBI**, because of its focus on intent, clarifying the means of preventing harm and the ways in which to promote good must be a crucial first step. In other words, we must understand where these deeply seeded intentions germinate from, and why? For example, if pressure builds up in some chemical reactor and the piping eventually blows up at a facility, closing the investigation after pointing to human error or neglect is not enough. Asking why a decision was made to neglect process safety fundamentals is what connects us to the intention behind the act. In doing so, we get a better understanding of the culture that drives that behavior. Asking the why questions opens up the possibility of re-evaluating deep-rooted norms, giving us the chance to realign our intentions. It is unfortunate that only in the aftermath of a dire incident or an accident do we tend to question our motives. Yet meaningful change need not come only from the outside. It can and often does happen when leaders have the foresight to understand the emerging business risks, the courage to galvanize change, and the wisdom to navigate the politics.

Leadership often goes through such realignments when a catastrophic event happens, such as a pandemic or a major accident. Trigger events, such as major disruptions or emerging risks, push businesses into a reactive mode where the symptoms get the attention, and not the root causes of the problem. Root causes, in this case, are deeper issues concerning business values, principles, and cultural norms, as opposed to symptoms that are at the procedural or practice level. The deeper the analysis, the more profound the transformation.

When Indra K. Nooyi took over as the CEO of PepsiCo, there were profound societal trends demanding healthier products. PepsiCo was losing the battle. She came in acutely aware of the challenges ahead. She had a burning desire to transform PepsiCo's core business model into one that contributes to society. To accomplish that, she had to work hard to realign business values, principles, and deeply-held cultural norms. In her 12 years as CEO, she turned the company around with her Performance with Purpose (PwP) initiative, which focused on four sustainability pillars: financial, health, environmental, and talent.

Co-authoring a *Harvard Business Review* article, Nooyi wrote: "Our social responsibility had to evolve away from corporate philanthropy and toward a deep sense of purpose that would also drive shareholder value. We needed to change the way we made money—not just give away some of the money we earned".[1]

When leaders start to redefine their values and principles to produce products or services with the intent to do no harm, then, and only then, organizations can focus their energies on facilitating the public interest and safeguarding the environment. The result is a new business paradigm: **MBI.**

MBI Principles provide a roadmap for organizations willing to embrace alignment with purposeful outcomes. And if that is the intent, then there are some fundamental questions every **MBI**-driven leader should ask their team:

1. Is our enterprise doing everything to protect the lives of its constituents?

2. How does each business manager plan on preserving the dignity of stakeholders?

3. Are our everyday decisions based on reason and rationality?

4. Are we managing wealth equitably for all stakeholders?

5. What measures are we enacting to safeguard and preserve the future for generations to come?

These principles represent commitments that **MBI** practitioners must embed in their decision-making processes at every level of the organization:

Principle

Preservation of Life translates into the safeguarding of human life from anything that threatens it, like workplace-related violence or sickness, and harm arising from exposure to hazardous working conditions or chemicals. We do see aspects of this principle with paid sick leave, workplace health and safety, ergonomic workspaces, and even work-life balance. The essence of this principle is instituting a concerted effort to care for and protect all life at a minimum, within the ecosystem the organization belongs in.

Principle

Preservation of Dignity translates into the safeguarding of human dignity from anything that degrades it, like labor commoditization, child and slave labor, income inequity, exploitation, degradation, and the deprivation of rights, etc. Something as simple as the acknowledgement of stakeholders, as such, qualifies them as being given the dignity of being seen. The essence of this principle is instituting a concerted effort to care for and protect human dignity at a minimum, within the ecosystem the organization belongs in.

Principle 3

Preservation of Reason is the safeguarding of the collective rationality and the related behaviors that result from it. It is being mindful of self-interest vs the interest of the other or of the many others; of respecting dissent by listening to varying perspectives; and of being aware of the biases in authority and their impact on individuals. Individual or collective reasoning can be many things to many people, but for our purposes, it is tied to the outcomes of bringing about the greater good at a minimum, within the ecosystem the organization belongs in.

Principle 4

Preservation of Wealth is centered around holistic financial wellness for the system. It is a respectful acknowledgement of where it came from, and the hard work undergone to bring it to its current place. To utilize wealth in a just manner, maintaining it and multiplying it for the benefit of as many as possible is a responsibility that is shouldered by every generation that takes on the charge. The essence of this principle is instituting a concerted effort to care for and protect the financial wellness of all stakeholders at a minimum, within the ecosystem the organization belongs in.

Principle 5

Preservation of the Future entails the conservation of our natural resources, natural habitats, and biodiversity for the continual benefit of all living beings. It is being mindful of the delicate balance nature has instilled on earth for its long-term sustainability. The essence of this principle is directly tied to the stewardship of the environment and preserving it for our future generations. It also encompasses the preservation of knowledge through investing in training, succession planning, mentoring and coaching, and maintaining social safety-nets through strong public and private partnerships.

In my client engagements over the years, I have found that small incremental steps to introducing the concepts behind **MBI** creates deeper meaning for achieving purposeful outcomes. The starting point, however, is for the organization's leadership to be open to critical self-reflection, analyzing existing emotional, cognitive, and behavioral dysfunctionality, and committing to balanced transformation for realigning their products and services for the greater good of society, promoting good and preventing harm.

Organic Valley is a good example of a company that promotes good by producing products that are beneficial to society. They are an independent cooperative of organic farmers based in La Farge, Wisconsin. The company's 30-plus year journey is inspiring on many levels. In the 1980s, the region's agricultural sector was struggling to survive against an onslaught of industrial chemical farming operations. Over 700 farmers lost their businesses to this global capitalistic force. There were two options on the table for the local farmers: either hop on the corporate farming bandwagon, or go bust.

For George Siemon, a local farmer who firmly believed in the holistic benefits of organic farming, selling out was not an option. It would have meant destroying the land and greatly disturbing the life cycle and rhythms of the natural world; inhibiting or destroying the habitat of mammals, birds, and insects.

If Siemon decided to passively give up or give in, he could lose his family heritage and organic farming roots. The future he envisioned for the preservation of the land for the next generation was at stake. It took wisdom on his part to understand the consequences of moving away from the practice of organic farming. Too many farmers had abandoned the traditional farming methods for commercial gain. The effect of industrialized farming threatened the entire natural ecosystem, including human life. It took courage on Siemon's part to stick to his values: non-GMO production, animal protection, sustainability, locally-focused and high quality products, and collaborations with like-minded farmers.

By bringing together other regional farmers into a cooperative, he unwittingly enacted **MBI** to realize his purpose. Organic Valley's website states: "There had to be a better way—a more sustainable way—to continue farming like we always had. In a way that protects the land, animals, economy and people's health. And that's how our farmer-owned cooperative was born."[2]

What started as seven local farmers banding together in 1988 has now grown into 2,000 cooperative members in 34 states. The company has consistent annual sales of $1.1 billion. Siemon's resolve required courage, wisdom, and temperance. These are three attributes forming the core of an **MBI** practitioner's psyche. The **MBI** state of mind can readily be found in such successful organizations, whose leaders enact their consciousness to build holistic business models.

The opposite is true for organizational leaders that do not have the courage, wisdom, or temperance to stay the course of fulfilling their intended purpose. Individuals who have been diagnosed with myopia have difficulty reading road signs and seeing distant objects clearly. The unfortunate outcome of this distortion in vision is short-sightedness. The same is true for organizational bodies, if their mission is self-serving, focused only on today, without a thought for tomorrow; the consequences of which, sooner or later, negatively affects their license to operate, their profit margins, and their environment.

It is this myopia that is the cause of the derailment of the US free enterprise market system. The pressure from capitalistic forces is so great to produce short-term profitability that even the most ardent entrepreneurs are held hostage by the tunnel vision of shareholder self-interest.

Take the tech start-up Etsy. They began as a small Brooklyn-based online artisanal marketplace. Etsy sold hand-crafted goods produced by micro-entrepreneur craftsmen; thereby providing them with an income they normally would not receive. The company embodied **MBI Principles** by providing its suppliers opportunities for **wealth, dignity,** and a **future**. They offered disenfranchised local artisans a platform, providing them with a fighting chance to earn a living next to market goliaths such as Amazon and Walmart.

Etsy emphasized its position as a company that put its social-driven mission before profits. It acquired a B Corporation certificate, which obliged it to submit annual proof that it met rigorous standards of social and environmental performance, accountability, and transparency. By early 2015, Etsy had gone public with a valuation of $1.8 billion and raised $237 million in IPO proceeds. It had 1.5 million active sellers and 22.6 million active buyers.

A few years later, Black-And-White Capital, a hedge fund; indifferent to the cause of helping local artisans increase their financial status, and fueled by a desire to increase profits, bought a majority of Etsy's shares to launch an aggressive buyout campaign. They succeeded in ousting the CEO and wasted no time in restructuring the company. They also forfeited Etsy's B Corporation status; which was a sign of the organization's commitment to balancing purpose and profit. B Corporation companies are legally required to consider the impact of their decisions on their workers, customers, suppliers, community, and the environment.

With the new management taking over, the value was no longer a unique platform for artisans; it was profitability. The company regressed in its operational philosophy, as it reclassified itself from B Corp to a general corporation. Two years after the takeover, although there were fluctuations, revenue and profits continued to show growth. Shareholders were happy. It did not seem to matter that they were not legally required to consider the impact of their decisions on their workers, customers, suppliers, community, and the environment. It will be interesting to see what compromising stakeholders for the profitability of shareholders does for Etsy.

Since organizations are made up of individuals, whose collective psyche and behavior seep into and form the organizational ethos, the challenge then becomes how to interpret the collective psyche of its executives, middle managers, and frontline supervisors. I believe the answer lies in the application of Al-Ghazali's model to the collective organizational ethos.

Al Ghazali's work on the human psyche was originally published in Arabic nearly a millennium ago. I am still fascinated by his perspective on optimal human performance. He argued that there are three systems that govern human character: emotional, behavioral, and cognitive. All three, when balanced and harmonized, create a just human being. It is only through the balancing of the three systems that we can achieve the recalibration and realignment of our sense of purpose that induces systemic fairness and justice. When actions are balanced in all three realms, what transpires is justice; a self-conscious realignment, in sync with the purpose of preventing harm and promoting good, based on equity and reciprocity. The Ghazali mindset is cultivated with consciousness and sincere effort, but it also requires systems thinking.

Imagine driving into a town with no road demarcations (i.e. yellow or white lines), stop signs or traffic lights. Top that off with no police presence. Would you drive under such conditions? In a bustling city, most people would think twice before driving on such a road. They might be a bit more open to driving on such a road if it is located in some remote area with little to no traffic. Chances are you would not come across a road like this in cities, or even most townships on our planet. In actuality, the majority of all transportation infrastructure operates under a globally consistent traffic management system. This system works because there is a common 'transportation language' that is equally understood worldwide: signs, symbols, lights and speed limits, registration procedures for vehicles, and licensing protocols for drivers. Similarly, Al-Ghazali provides the components for understanding our own psyche. Once realized, our subconscious and conscious mind begins to speak that common language for developing a more just and fair sense of purpose.

Every system has a specific set of directives to establish the general system logic for conformance. Adherence to **MBI**'s five principles is essential for integrating purposefulness into organizational performance outcomes. The principles create consistency and are broad enough to facilitate a variety of strategic and tactical business imperatives. Collectively, they constitute a universal code of conduct. A key facilitator for the **MBI** journey is a systems thinking frame of reference. This reference plays heavily in a leader's comprehension of an **MBI**-centric approach to organizational development. Systems thinkers are best positioned to fully leverage **MBI** Principles because of their understanding of the following six attributes:

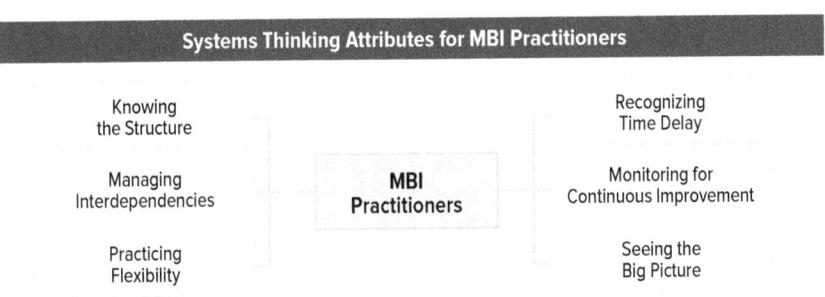

Knowing the Structure of a system is understanding how the various components fit together for optimal performance. Components can be defined as underlying policies and procedures, values, mental models, communication flows, and performance management systems. Recognizing the interconnectedness of the components facilitates awareness of the system's dynamics, enabling us to comprehend system behavior, and identify its boundaries.

Managing Interdependencies is about understanding interconnectedness of the parts of the whole. It requires a shift away from linear thinking to a circular one. Circular interdependencies have multiple touch points within and outside of all the parts that collectively make up the whole. Realizing that to tamper with one aspect of a business in an isolated fashion will have consequences for other aspects of that business is the first step in untangling the complexities when it comes to inducing change in a system.

Practicing Flexibility is the ability to modify strategy and operations in response to uncertain or unpredictable circumstances. This is needed in times when behavioral change is warranted to turnaround and transform business. Flexibility is not only about surviving or thriving in existing situations, it is also about the adaptability to explore emerging knowledge for solving problems. Flexible leaders, therefore, have the intellectual capacity to look at a situation from a variety of angles and from various points of view without preferences or bias.

Recognizing Time Delay is knowing that when an action is taken within a complex, dynamic system, the outcome of that action may not be seen for some time. The gauging of when results should begin to be seen and felt needs to be built into change management plans. For example, when going to the gym for a week to radically shape one's body, the results will not be seen that week, no matter how much you train. The process is prolonged and the body goes through aches and pains before starting to show signs of improvement. Similarly, sustained and consistent effort is needed, along with perseverance and patience, for long-term transformation.

Monitoring for Continuous Improvement throughout the process can be built into systems to evaluate in real-time and at finite intervals, for not all results are seen or realized immediately. Evaluation then should take on a layered approach as well, which allows refinement and fine-tuning from multiple snapshots in time. Continuous evaluation and monitoring is not a separate function, but rather an ongoing process, built within the system.

Seeing the Big Picture is awareness of the current contexts within which the business exists (economic, social, geopolitical, and environmental), the interconnectivity between each facet, and any impact or influence on the business itself. The challenges leaders face on a daily basis are no longer simple and straightforward; yet the solutions must satisfy many and not create more problems for tomorrow. To be successful in the contemporary world, the ability to systematically work through problems are fast becoming prerequisite skills.

In the end, the long-term sustainability of a change initiative such as **MBI** rides on the ability of its practitioner to espouse systems thinking characteristics in conjunction with industry expertise. Attempts to haphazardly change a system—without a thought-out approach, void of multiple viewpoints, and without consultation—will only be a short-lived or cursory change. Transformative change requires sustained bilateral persistence and a collective understanding of the dynamic interdependencies, before embarking on such a journey, for long-term change to get rooted in organizations.

The perils we face today—from the polarization of thought and numbness towards suffering, to the total disregard of environmental degradation—require an integrated systems approach to change. After all, our planet is a closed-looped system. Any attempt to fix its issues without a fuller understanding of the interdependencies of its subsystems will have detrimental effects on all inhabitants of this planet.

> **?** Before moving on to the next chapter, I would request you to pause and ask yourself the following questions:
>
> **1.** Is the sense of purpose for my organization well-defined?
>
> **2.** As we realign to become a company of tomorrow, what sort of questions are being asked in boardrooms and executive meetings?
>
> **3.** Is anyone asking questions about organizational purpose? If so, what is their intent?

Chapter 3

The Knowledge of Self

> Character is not identified with an action, a faculty, or knowledge; rather it is the disposition of the soul from which actions emerge...
>
> — Al-Ghazali,
> 11th century Sufi mystic

BUSINESSES TODAY FACE unprecedented complexity and volatility. The intensity of economic, social, environmental, and political forces almost always create turbulence. 21st century businesses are expected to step up and be a force of good for the societies they operate in. This requires clarity of vision and organizational purpose where leaders are seen as just brokers, advocating for mission critical issues such as environmental stewardship and climate change, social equity and justice, and income and wealth parity. Taking on this role will require intimately knowing the collective organizational self. This is where Al-Ghazali's model of the human psyche can help.

I was introduced to Al-Ghazali (c.1058–1111) through my exposure to dignitaries from Asia and Africa at the IMF and the World Bank in the 1990s. Commonly referred to as the greatest revivalist of his time, Al-Ghazali was a jurist, theologian, philosopher, and mystic known for his invaluable contributions to the systematization of the Islamic creed. To this day, he remains an influential intellectual.

His comprehensive philosophy encompassed social reform, individual ethics, and moral responsibility. In the early 21st century, some of his seminal works were reintroduced to the west. Committed to refining and understanding my own inner workings on a deeper level, I delved into his writings on human behavior and psychology.

In his book, Alchemy of Happiness, Al-Ghazali identified three systems that make up the human psyche: emotional, behavioral, and cognitive. According to him, if the human psyche is balanced, the intellect is endowed with the ability to think critically; self-analyze; and reason. Collectively, these three abilities form our moral compass, influencing our thought process (intentions) and the resulting behaviors (actions) to induce a sense of justice within us.[3]

It is the sense of justice of a leader that brings deeper purpose to the organization, inspires and elevates people, upholds moral values, and actively engages in questions of right and wrong. That, in turn, defines the organizational culture: the values and principles, beliefs and practices, rules of engagement, and the resulting strategic imperatives. The knowledge of self is, therefore, a critical first step in calibrating our compass to point to the two **MBI** proverbial poles: doing no harm and promoting good.

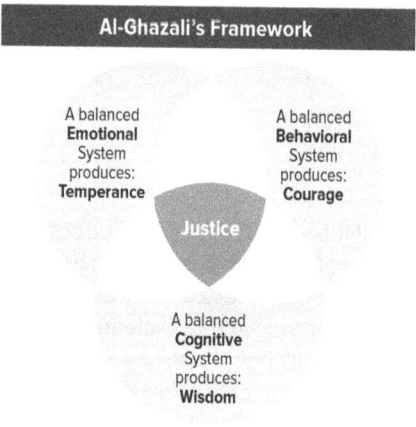

Based on Al-Ghazali's framework, I visualize my own psyche as a tire swing hanging from a tree. There are three of me sitting on the tire: an emotional me; a behavioral me; and a cognitive me. There are two opposing forces that are active on my swing: my impulsiveness and my responsiveness. The goal is to keep the swing relatively stable, in a state of dynamic equilibrium. The impulsive force in me tends to push the swing away from its resting position, thereby disturbing my mind's equilibrium. The responsive force in me tends to pull the swing back to the resting position to restore my composure. Achieving equilibrium, in this scenario, would be relatively easy if I only exert an equal amount of responsiveness to impulsiveness, in order to stay in a state of dynamic equilibrium. An added challenge comes from the excessive or the deficient state of my emotional, behavioral, and cognitive systems. If any of these systems are imbalanced, circularity is added to the motion of the proverbial swing, and all we get is a spinning effect.

Al-Ghazali's work was limited to individuals, but it can be applied to the organizational psyche as well. Since organizations are made up of individuals, their collective psyche dictates the direction of the swing and the amount of spin involved. When organizational systems are assessed using Al-Ghazali's model, the results are eye-opening. The following is a brief synopsis of what I have learned over the years:

The Emotional System

A sound emotional system leads to temperance in organizational decision-making.

Emotional System Characteristics (Love & Pleasure Centric)		
Excessive (+)	Balanced (0)	Deficient (-)
Gluttony	Temperance	Lethargy
Characteristics: • Shamelessness • Foulness	Characteristics: • Modesty • Contentment	Characteristics: • Spinelessness • Dishonor

Excessiveness within the Emotional system creates organizational cultures that are driven by self-indulgence, where it is acceptable to earn profits driven solely through greed. In 2018, the *Intercept* published a report, 'How Wall Street Drove Public Pensions Into Crisis and Pocketed Billions in Fees', which highlighted "how public pensions squander tens of billions of dollars each year on risky, poor-performing alternative investments like hedge funds". That is a perfect example of avarice!

The report goes on to indicate that "[w]hen, in 2017, the Pew Charitable Trusts looked at 73 of the country's largest public pensions, researchers found that a full 25 percent of the pension money was invested in these high-fee alternatives."

It also states that "[t]he founders of hedge funds and private equity partnerships tend to be Wall Street refugees who were making millions a year working for Goldman Sachs or Morgan Stanley, but figured out that they could make even more in alternatives. The key to that wealth is the '2 and 20,' as it is called within the industry. Hedge funds and private equity alike typically collect a 2 percent management fee ($2 million for every $100 million invested) and then take 20 percent of any profits before distributing them to investors. Double that $100 million over a 10-year period, and reward yourself with a $20 million performance fee. The worst aspect of the '2 and 20' is even if a $5 billion fund makes no money for its investors, it still walks away with $100 million in management fees."[4]

Keep in mind these are pension funds for teachers, firemen and policemen, pillars of our civil society; public servants, now labeled as essential workers.

> **Which of the five MBI preservation principles do you think these hedge fund managers are breaking with impunity, in the case above?**
>
> a. Life, dignity and wealth
> b. Reason and future
> c. All five preservation principles
> d. None of the above

On the flip side, deficiency within the Emotional System creates cultures that are driven by lethargy. They continue to maintain the status-quo, even in the face of daunting evidence for the need to change. These are dinosaurs from another era, refusing to evolve.

On March 1, 2020, Bethany Barnes, an investigative reporter for the Florida-based *Tampa Bay Times*, published an explosive year-long report. Her piece was about GardaWorld's 19 fatal crashes, attributed to their badly maintained armored fleet. As I read through the report, I was baffled by the utter depravity of the company's Emotional System.

GardaWorld is the largest privately-owned security services company in the world, with a workforce of over 92,000. They have a brilliant success story of exponential financial growth and global expansion, if looked at purely from a financial perspective. However, according to Barnes' investigation, the company is an abject horror story of greed and callousness when it comes to safeguarding the lives of its own workforce and the greater community it operates in.[5]

In a recent interview, GardaWorld CEO Stephan Crétier said his mission is to conquer the world. For a global security company that has grown exponentially, I can see how this single-minded focus on 'conquering the world' can shift leadership's attention to growth at any cost. Cutting corners to hit revenue targets seems like a cultural norm at GardaWorld. So what if a few lives have been lost due to poorly maintained trucks and equipment? Maintaining the status-quo seems to be business as usual for this enterprise.

The Behavioral System
A healthy behavioral system leads to courage in organizational decision-making.

Behavioral System Characteristics (Anger & Pain Centric)		
Excessive (+)	Balanced (0)	Deficient (-)
Recklessness	**Courage**	**Cowardice**
Characteristics: • Boasting • Excessive Risk-Taking	Characteristics: • High-mindedness • Moderation	Characteristics: • Apprehension • Appeasement

Excessiveness within the Behavioral System creates organizational cultures that are driven by recklessness, where the consequences of negative behavior are repeatedly ignored in order to meet shareholder expectations. The British Petroleum Company's inability to heed the warning signs about unsafe conditions and potentially catastrophic health consequences at their Deepwater Horizon drilling rig is a great example of this type of imbalance. Many lives and livelihoods were lost or destroyed. In addition, entire ecosystems and tens of thousands of miles of coastline were irreparably damaged. A federal board investigation concluded that a last-ditch safety device on the underwater well had multiple failures. It was never tested properly.

Similarly, deficiency within the Behavioral System creates organizational cultures that are driven by cowardice. This is when leaders exhibit complacency and take a cavalier attitude when confronted with challenging issues and information. In such cases, responsibilities are neglected and disregarded. The Boeing 737 Max plane fiasco revealed the cowardice and avarice on the part of the leadership team. The company was wholly responsible for 346 deaths, yet no one had the courage to stand up and question the consequences of selling short on safety standards. Hundreds of internal emails released by Boeing to Congress and the Federal Aviation Administration revealed general discomfort and concern among staffers about design issues with the plane. The most revealing was an employee's instant message: "This airplane is designed by clowns who in turn are supervised by monkeys."

The company seemed more interested in appeasing its shareholders than squarely facing the consequences of its actions. It took Boeing a year to oust its CEO. He was denied severance, but still walked away with 60 million dollars. To add insult to injury, the new CEO is part of the old guard. He was on the Board of Directors when the decision was made to create the retro-fitted 737 Max plane.

Instead, to ensure the public's safety, they should have dedicated funding to properly design a plane. Despite the ultimate responsibility of the Board for this colossal failure, the majority remain in power. They were there before the announcement to sell the retrofitted planes. Do you seriously believe their corporate culture and attitude towards customer safety will change?

The Cognitive System
A balanced Cognitive System is one where organizational wisdom is leveraged in decision-making.

Cognitive System Characteristics (Knowledge & Reason-Centric)		
Excessive (+)	Balanced (0)	Deficient (-)
Deception	**Wisdom**	**Foolishness**
Characteristics: • Slyness • Chicanery	Characteristics: • Good Planning • Balanced Judgement	Characteristics: • Stupidity • Imprudence

Excessiveness within the Cognitive System leads to organizational cultures that are driven by deceit: roles, responsibilities and information is misrepresented, hoarded or hidden. The electronic and tech industries' unintelligible 'Terms of Use' is a good example of excessiveness of the Cognitive System, misleading consumers into surrendering their privacy when using their devices. A joint collaboration between Northeastern University, Chicago, and the Imperial College of London examined the data sharing activities of 81 different types of smart devices commonly found in people's homes. An astounding 72 of the 81 devices shared data with third-party tech vendors located around the world, not related to the original manufacturer. Data such as IP addresses, device specifications and configurations, usage habits, and location data is usually shared as a plaintext file without any sort of encryption at all. Our homes are now leaking data and anyone eavesdropping could easily get access to the smart device user's identity, location, and behavior.

Shortcomings within the Cognitive System also produce corporate cultures driven by foolishness, where in spite of overwhelming scientific evidence, common sense is abandoned as businesses rationalize their goals and behaviors in pursuit of maximizing short-term economic gains. The coal industry is a good example of this irrational behavior.

When wisdom, courage, and temperance come together, justice is the result.

Before we dive into fixing the organization, let us start with a little inward reflection. One of the great Sufi poets from Punjab, Bulleh Shah, spoke about humanity's struggle to understand itself. Here are a few lines translated from one of his poems:

> *By reading books we gain knowledge*
> *Yet we never spend time knowing our souls*
> *Our thoughts are shaped by externalities*
> *Yet we never contemplate what the heart holds*
> *We have reached the limitless skies*
> *But we have failed to reach our heart's inner folds*

In the context of **MBI**, it is inward reflection that initiates the ability to self-regulate our code of conduct in alignment with the greater good, facilitating public interest and safeguarding the environment. That adherence to a code of conduct for the greater good is only cultivated in organizations when the behavioral, emotional, and cognitive aspects of their leaders' psyche achieve balance in understanding the essence of what the greater good entails. The deeper the understanding of that balance, the deeper the commitment for the greater good.

In today's world, we witness an ever-growing list of corporations and businesses that have lost their sense of purpose. In the quest for amassing wealth, we frequently deceive our customers through marketing gimmicks, recklessly expose our workers to harmful conditions, and unfairly enrich our shareholders at the expense of everyone else. Indifferent to the plight of communities, we degrade sacred lands, pollute waterways and deplete natural resources. These are all clear signs of a deficient collective psyche begging for realignment and recalibration. Clearly, the incredible imbalance in society today is unsustainable.

> **?** Before moving on to the next chapter, I would request you to pause and ask yourself the following questions:
>
> **1** When was the last time you engaged in meaningful self-assessment?
>
> **2** How do you solicit feedback to gain a better understanding of your personal leadership style?

Chapter 4

Retrofitting the System

> We can't save the world by playing by the rules, because the rules have to be changed. Everything needs to change, and it has to start today.
>
> — **Greta Thunberg,**
> Climate Activist

MBI IS NOT just a transformative system of personal change management, as discussed in the previous chapter. **MBI** requires top-down commitment and bottom-up engagement. This chapter is an overview of what that commitment and engagement looks like.

In my years of consulting, I have observed several sustainable strategies to jumpstart transformative change. Almost always, they were driven by a sense of purpose, and the leadership's deep-rooted intention to change the status quo, which had a chokehold on progress. Without a yearning to change from the top brass, change would not appear automatically at the lower tiers. Like the story of the dog who, while sitting on a porch, would occasionally howl. When the owner was asked about the dog's reason for howling, she replied, "It is sitting on a nail." Amused by the scenario, a guest asked, "Well, if it is sitting on a nail, why does it not get up and move over to another spot?" The owner shrugged her shoulders and replied, "I guess the nail does not hurt bad enough."

If the message from the top does not galvanize the workforce, change is short-lived. Infusing **MBI** becomes an exercise in aligning, educating, and enabling the board, first and foremost, followed by executive leadership, and then finally the entire workforce. If the current state of our planet's environmental, social, and political conditions are not hurting your organization in a negative way, then **MBI** may not be of any value. However, if you are a compassionate and concerned corporate citizen and want to explore avenues to aid you in making meaningful change, **MBI** will offer intrinsic value.

A truly transformative journey starts with connecting one's consciousness, morally and ethically, with a higher purpose than the self. With higher purpose comes the recognition of response-ability; the agility and ability to respond to situations that hold us accountable such as governance and management. As explained in Chapter 3, if our swing is not in a state of dynamic equilibrium—where our emotional, behavioral, and cognitive systems are working harmoniously—our psyche and subsequent decisions and actions will be imbalanced. Just as the tires of our cars tread unevenly if the wheels are not aligned, when these three systems are not centered, our intentions become blurry and misguided. An imbalanced organizational psyche can and does justify any detrimental action, as long as short-term profitability is achieved.

Calibrating intentions requires a systems thinking mindset, and a reset from the old paradigm. In the new **MBI** configuration, a system's features such as goal orientation, inputs and outputs, transformation, regulation, hierarchy, and differentiation all align to benefit the greater good. Leadership's upgraded mindset consists of the wisdom, courage, and temperance to guide the decision-making process that influences every level of the organization in a positive manner. Transformation, however, can only materialize when:

1. Leadership's aspirations extend beyond short-term monetary gains to take stakeholders into consideration.
2. Everyone in the organization truly understands the need for change and personally feels the impact of the products or services they offer on the lives of customers and the environment.

About five years ago, my team received a request from a global client to help them with an organizational transformation effort in Africa. Since the company had some contractor fatalities in North America, the leadership was determined to initiate a change campaign. A worldwide integrated management system focused on safety was part of that initiative. It was an attempt to initiate global measures and standards to protect the safety and health of their workforce (i.e. **Preservation of Life**). Having had some limited success with their North American assets, they turned their attention to the African business units by way of a policy directive, which was issued with the expectation of full compliance within six months.

Two years had gone by without any progress. In this time, two attempts were made to implement the directive with lots of time and money spent on the efforts. Both attempts yielded dismal results. The Houston-based headquarter's (HQ) implementation team was under intense pressure to deliver. That is when my team was called in to fix the problem. I sat down with the corporate team to get a better understanding of the situation. I was told that the African business units were being obtuse and non-cooperative. Being the biggest revenue generating block for the company, there were not many levers that the struggling HQ team could pull to coerce them into compliance. Their approach was very top-down and hierarchical.

Before taking on the project, I also wanted to hear from the African team; to get their side of the story. When I had my conference call, I was told the HQ team came across as pushy, shoehorning their agenda, with no regard to the needs of the local stakeholders.

As my team and I completed our initial assessment, it was apparent that the biggest challenge was not the alignment on what was needed (i.e. a safety focused management system); it was the lack of understanding of why it was needed. As a result, they failed to create buy-in at an emotional level with their stakeholders. In order to do it right the third time around, we had to modify their loosely framed four-step management systems cycle. That was the genesis of the **MBI** transformation cycle shown below.

Table 1: MBI Four-Step Iterative Transformation Cycle

Step 1: **Align** organizational leadership and management on why there is a need for change.

Step 2: **Educate** all levels of the organization on *why* the change is needed; *what* needs to be done differently; and who is going to do it.

Step 3: **Empower** how things will be done differently moving forward.

Step 4: **Monitor** performance against set criteria and realign based on results.

Our approach included a few additional components to the deployment plan. A high-level summary of the approach is presented in the table below. The check marks indicate aspects of **MBI** that we included in our approach.

Table 2: Modified Deployment Plan

Original Approach	System Hierarchy	MBI Approach
Why Do It? • Conformance to policy at any cost • Commitment to work environment free of harm		**Why Do It?** ✔ Preserve Life at any cost ✔ Shared understanding of the expected benefits
What Needs To Be Done? • Realign our vision, redefine our business principles and strategies objectives • Optimized value (i.e. cost and risk)	Policy (Why?) Expectations & Guidelines (What?)	**What Needs To Be Done?** ✔ Instill system thinking mindset • Realign our vision, redefine our business principles and strategies objectives • Optimized value (i.e. cost and risk)
How It Will Be Done? • Translate "Policy" into operations outcomes • Leverage existing processes and tools	Standards & Practices (How?)	**How It Will Be Done?** ✔ Translate "Preservation of Life" into operations outcomes • Leverage existing processes and tools

Let us briefly look at the four check-marked statements in **Table 2**. Leadership's ability to understand the *why* and then turn around and meaningfully articulate it in order to elicit the needed emotional buy-in is a critical first step. Similarly, for the stakeholders—in this case, the workforce in Africa—the ability to see the initiative as part of the whole (i.e. a system) is critical to their internalizing the concept.

A great mentor of mine explained the concept of 'internalizing' with a beautiful story.

One day, a professor was driving with his three-year-old daughter to the store. On the way there, the little girl asked her father, "Daddy why did you stop the car at the traffic light?" In a rather educational tone, the professor responded, "Because the light is red, and red means stop". The little girl queried, "But why?". The professor replied, "So the policeman does not give us a ticket". The little girl, still unable to internalize the message, asked again, "Why?". The professor paused a bit to think and then said, "Well, honey, because crossing a red light is very dangerous". The little girl, who had yet to emotionally buy into this rule, asked again, "Why?" By this time, they had already pulled into the parking lot of the store. The professor shut the car off, unbuckled his seat belt, turned around, looked her in the eye and said, "Well, young lady, because we cannot hurt people. Would you like to be hurt yourself?"

She looked down at herself, looked back up again, and with a pensive tone said, "No!" The professor continued, "Just like you, other people also do not want to be hurt. We should love people as we love our own self".

The little girl thought for a bit and then came back with, "Why do you love for people what you love for yourself, daddy?" The professor smiled and got out of the car. He helped her out, held her hand and, as they walked into the store, replied, "We love people the same as we love ourselves, because we are all equal".

As I finished narrating the story at one of my workshops, I could sense the audience thinking and connecting the dots.

MBI is about connecting the dots to understand the *why*s. Protecting the safety and health of the workforce can have many different layers of *why*s. The most superficial one is one of compliance. The most deepest one is of the universal value of life. The reason we modified their original approach, outlined in **Table 2**, was because their why stopped at compliance (i.e. conforming to policy). There was no connectivity to any higher cause. Compliance alone does not produce a galvanizing sense of purpose, does it?

Preservation of Life is so much more than a slogan concocted in a boardroom. We had to modify the original *why* from being superficially focused on the policy directive and sloganeering, to a more succinct **Preservation of Life** principle, coupled with shared understanding of the mutual benefits gained from it. Benefits that entail aspects such as dignity of work, respect, equality, and uplifting local communities. We had to also modify the *what* to add a systems thinking mindset in the workforce, so they could relate to the bigger picture and realize their important role in shaping it. Last but not least, we had to modify the *how* to give the workforce a common language around behavioral outcomes and get them to focus on shared goals, such as hazard awareness and recognition, and stop work authority (i.e. to stop work when you see something wrong).

To accomplish our goals, we conducted a series of facilitated workshops strategically placed at various intervals during the project. These workshops were conducted with the purpose to help the stakeholders (i.e business unit leaders, operational leads, and staff) better understand *why*, *what* and *how* best to move forward with **Preservation of Life** as the central theme. Since the nature of the workshops were meant to be collaborative, a combination of the stakeholder groups were brought together to create stimulating discussions on various topics.

A sample of discussion questions are presented below in **Table 3**.

Table 3: Workshop Discussion Questions

Strategic Questions	Tactical Questions
• Why does Preservation of Life matter? • Do we have the clear and shared understanding of the expected benefits? • What are we currently doing to safeguard safety and health? • Are we doing it well?	• How do we realign our vision, or redefine our business principles and strategic objectives? • How do we optimize value, and at what cost or risk? • How will Preservation of Life translate into production and operations outcomes? • Do we have the right skillset? • How much of the existing processes and tools can we leverage?

Leaders helped shape the discussion around governance, highlighting issues such as: oversight and accountability, roles and responsibilities, performance management, rewards and incentives. The operational leads helped in adding color to the operational aspects, such as: authority, goals-setting, key performance indicators, performance measurements, skills and expertise, capacity, standards and procedures. The staff members gave us great insight into day-to-day tasks and activities, required and anticipated competencies, and the usages of tools.

As a result of the modified **MBI** approach and the facilitated workshops that followed, we took them from 'the policeman is going to give us a ticket' to 'we love for you what we love for ourselves'. Although that was the beginning of the transformative journey, a few revealing perspectives were unearthed:

1. The more leadership expressed empathy for the staff's needs and leaned in to listen, the better they were able to identify, understand and manage the staff's point-of-view and, consequently, their own expectations.

2. As they spent more time with leadership, the staff felt more empowered to express their thoughts.

At the end of the day, it boiled down to the need for bidirectional change. The corporate team was hellbent on forcing top-down change, all the while resisting change on their end. Forcing the local stakeholders to care about preservation of **life** meant they themselves ought to have cared about **life** by honoring **dignity** and respecting **reason** of the stakeholders to fortify their **future**. But they did not! For the staff, preserving **life**, by means of a management system, was just not good enough initially. They wanted a more everlasting change; one that promised the assurance of **dignity** of work and respect for upholding their **reason** for a common **future** where they had equity and justice for all.

For this particular client, the change process demanded a multilayered approach to addressing the staff's needs. Although it took time to get everyone on board, once management understood the multidimensionality of the initiative, and its overall effects for the greater good, implementing the needed change was accomplished smoothly. The staff's attitude towards management was no longer adversarial in nature. Instead, it was a dramatic shift from the old paradigm to one where they embraced the much needed management systems overhaul.

In my closing meeting with the client, it had become apparent to the HQ team why the first two attempts had failed. Understanding the **MBI** framework from a systems thinking mindset, coupled with the facilitated workshops to take a deeper dive into the transformation, and connecting the dots between the **five principles** had made all the difference.

MBI transformations require an investment of 'time and money' in the form of expertise, funding, and infrastructure, over and above the normal costs of conducting ongoing business operations. What I have discovered is that, in order for organizations to succeed with an **MBI** transformation, their efforts must encompass the following aspects:

- The MBI philosophy and its applicability are understood and integrated into processes.

- A life-cycle approach is taken to ascertain the impact of products and services on the environment and society.

- Identification of exactly who will be impacted, and to what extent.

- The players involved in managing change are acknowledged and leveraged.

- Factoring time at every level and stage of the planning process, and not just in terms of when objectives will be met, but also how time-sensitive dependencies across transformational milestones are addressed.

In my engagement with global organizations, I have also learned that the following critical success factors need to be present for transformational change to happen:

1. A strong and visible executive champion.

2. A vision for transformation that is realistic and helps ensure that the journey to its realization can be completed.

3. Adequate resources.

4. Flexibility to address and respond to opportunities and risks associated with a wide range of circumstances.

In the following chapters, we will discuss each of **MBI**'s five principles to further explore the *why*, *what* and *how*.

Chapter 5
The First Principle: The Preservation of Life

> Actions are lifeless forms, but the presence of an inner reality of sincerity within them is what endows them life-giving spirits.
>
> — ibn 'Atā Allāh,
> 13th century Egyptian Sufi Jurist

IT MAY BE hard to believe, but people are still dying on the job each day in the US. According to the US Bureau of Labor Statistics, a total of 5,250 workers died on the job in 2018. That is an average of more than 100 fatalities per week and more than 14 deaths per day. Out of 4,779 worker fatalities in the private sector, 21% were in construction.[6] In the coming months and years, as we start to accumulate more in-depth data on hazards faced by frontline workers due to the lack of personal protective equipment (PPE) during the COVID-19 pandemic, I am afraid we will see heavy casualties in the healthcare sector as well.

According to OSHA, the leading causes of worker deaths in the construction industry, not including highway collisions, included: falls, being struck by an object, electrocution, and being caught-in/between materials. In 2018, there were almost three million non-fatal workplace injuries and illnesses due to unsafe or unhealthy work conditions reported by private industry employers. An overwhelming majority of these accidents were attributed to hourly or contract workers. In the construction industry, in particular, workers tend to be migrants without official visas, which tragically seems to make them more expendable.[7] In 2020, the COVID-19 pandemic will further exacerbate these numbers.

The aptly named American Institute of Stress claimed that workplace stress cost the American economy some $300 billion each year. Additionally, work-related stress causes 120,000 deaths and results in $190 billion in healthcare costs annually.[8] According to the International Labour Organization (ILO), over two million workers die each year from unsafe or unhealthy working conditions. In spite of a clear human rights obligation to protect their well-being, workers around the world find themselves facing health crises. ILO estimates that one worker dies every 30 seconds from exposure to toxic industrial chemicals, pesticides, dust, radiation, and other hazardous substances.[9]

According to a recent report published by the Centers for Disease Control (CDC), "In 2017, nearly 38,000 persons of working age (16-64 years) in the United States died by suicide, which represents a 40% rate increase (12.9 per 100,000 population in 2000 to 18.0 In 2017) in less than two decades. Workers in the extraction (Mining, Quarrying, and Oil and Gas) and construction sectors are especially vulnerable to suicide. The transient nature of the work, along with low pay, tough schedules, and physical rigors, can lead to self-medication and substance abuse.[10]

The above statistics are shocking and, some might think, immoral. How can the so-called richest country in the world have such lax workplace practices and dangerous conditions that lead to disabilities, or worse, death?

In layman's terms, the **Preservation of Life** principle safeguards human life from anything that threatens it. Workplace-related violence, stress, sickness or harm arising from a number of factors, and exposure to hazardous chemicals and working conditions clearly fall into this category. The antidote is then mindfulness of workers' mental, physical, and social well-being.

The COVID-19 pandemic of 2020 overwhelmingly hurt hourly, part-time, gig and contract workers in America. Since most public venues such as retail, restaurants, and offices are shut down during such pandemics, these workers are the hardest hit. They are on the front line, the first to be let go, and the lowest paid. Their fear and uncertainty of future employment is real. Should these workers get employment protection?

While businesses were quick to accommodate their full-time workers during the COVID-19 outbreak, the same benefits were initially not extended to their hourly, low wage contractors. Until recently, most states excluded gig workers, freelancers, caregivers, and the self-employed from access to unemployment insurance (UI). Undocumented immigrants are also categorically ineligible. Twenty-seven states exclude full-time students from UI; a reality that has hurt many students working in the service sector. The US Bureau of Labor Statistics' data suggests that approximately 30% of workers in the lowest wage bracket have paid sick leave. But what about the remaining 70%? It is a basic human rights question that every CEO and shareholder needs to address. For we are, indeed, as strong as our weakest link. Essential workers, who were once taken for granted, are now seen as heroes of society, during the pandemic.

The **Preservation of Life** safeguards humanity from devastation and harmful practices on the part of unscrupulous entities. Practices that destroy natural habitats for other living species are also part of this commitment. This principle is the foundational stepping stone for putting into practice the four other **MBI Principles**. The sanctity of life, its preservation and safekeeping, is a universal truth.

A good example of the **Preservation of Life** principle is the parent-child relationship. Most mothers are willing to sacrifice everything to protect the safety and well-being of their child(ren). They will go to extreme measures to keep their children out of harm's way, both emotionally and physically. The parents collectively and instinctively provide a protective and nurturing environment for their child; which is embedded in the parent's DNA.

The same caring relationship could exist between organizations and their stakeholders, be it employees, customers, or community members. A recent article in the *Harvard Business Review* states: "If workers feel like they belong, companies reap substantial bottom-line benefits. High belongingness was linked to a whopping 56% increase in job performance, a 50% drop in turnover risk, and a 75% reduction in sick days. For a 10,000-person company, this would result in annual savings of more than $52 million."[11]

A sense of belonging and appreciation in the workplace leads to more than just a good collegial work atmosphere. Indeed, it allows employees to feel like they can be their authentic selves without fear of maltreatment or discrimination. This feeling of "belonging" also has a positive impact on performance, retention, growth, productivity, creativity, and collaboration.

When I first moved to Houston, I remember having a discussion with a client, Marc; who was a senior executive at a global oil and gas company. Marc shared a life-changing event early on in his career that forced him to reflect and reprioritize his original intentions. Until that moment, as a young production supervisor, Marc's focus had been purely on the production process, not safety. Although his organization talked about worker safety being the number one priority, the principle that was enforced was 'Production is King'. Employees were rewarded for increased output. As a result of this belief system, the underlying corporate culture was not of safety first, but of production at any cost.

To churn out product, Marc put his life on the line many times. One day, his luck ran out. He suffered a near-death experience when one of his sub-stations blew up. There was a massive explosion and his entire body caught on fire. That accident was entirely preventable had he only thought through the impact of his acute focus on 'product first'. Miraculously, he survived, and learned quite a few lessons from his harrowing experience:

1. The power of his organization's culture shaped the employees' expectations and perspective about safety.

2. A singular focus on production had to be reversed.

3. Safety must be ensured for all his team members.

4. His actions influenced his team more than his words.

Production is King became an impulsive force pushing his mind's proverbial swing away from its central resting position. Safety was no longer the priority. Each time he pushed to get production back on line, bypassing safety procedures, his actions became a little more reckless (excessive behavioral system, characterized by impulsiveness). He was knowingly neglecting the consequences of his actions (deficient emotional system, characterized by lethargy). He was counting on the reward to be greater than the risk he was taking, even if it meant risking his life (deficient cognitive system, characterized by foolishness).

The ripple effects of an occupational illness or injury are not just confined to personal health, it equally impacts social, and financial realms. At a social level, an injury, regardless of its magnitude, affects quality of life, self-esteem, self-confidence and family relationships. The cost of medical care and ongoing general expenses on a reduced income can very quickly deplete savings, forcing the victim to borrow money, taking out retirement funds, or worse, declaring bankruptcy in efforts to cope.

Marc was extremely lucky. In spite of a major setback due to an injury, he was able to make a full recovery and get back to work. He made a sincere commitment to make it his mission to transform his company's safety culture to one focused on **Preservation of Life**. But it was not easy to bring about the transformation. A concerted effort by parties at all organizational levels was required to alter and educate perspectives on safety prioritization. A comprehensive company-wide initiative was launched with the following key aspects:

- Strong, visible leadership and a clear mandate from the highest levels of the organization to provide the sponsorship and resources necessary to see the initiative through.

- A clear, corporate manifesto with a buy-in from executives and employees at every level to continuously improve the focus of management practices that value life.

- A heightened sense of awareness, at the highest levels of the organization, to uphold and promote governance principles and practices in alignment with the commitment.

- Alignment of structures, mechanisms, processes, and procedures to uphold and support the adoption of a new safety-first culture.

- Clearly defined and enforced accountabilities, up and down the chain of command, supporting safety practices.

- The use of safety infused performance-oriented metrics and measurements as a basis for decision-making and planning.

- A forward-looking outlook and bias toward personal and process safety.

A rudimentary application of this principle is seen in action at many organizations and throughout different industries. The emphasis typically tends to be placed on personal and process safety, but we know that **Preservation of Life** goes beyond physical safety. In fact, it encompasses a total commitment to workers' mental, physical, and social well-being. In its highest form, this principle goes beyond the confines of the organizational walls into the worker's home and the communities the organization serves and is a part of.

Table 4 offers a simple maturity assessment guide to evaluate your organization's current state of **Preservation of Life**. It serves as a good starting point to quickly determine the critical success factors needed to implement this at your organization. As you go through the assessment, I would like you to keep the following two questions in mind:

1. What are the accelerators and drivers for this principle at your organization?

2. Determine where your organization is on this chart. What are the inhibitors, challenges, and pitfalls that prevent advancement to the next stage?

Table 4: Preservation of Life - Maturity Assessment

Stage 0 Subpar	Stage 1 Reactive	Stage 2 Developing	Stage 3 Advance	Stage 4 Leading
Preservation of Life is not a critical component of the company's philosophy. Harm to life or health is a natural by-product of doing business that needs to be managed.	Protection of the safety and health of employees is primarily through policy directives. As incidents and accidents occur, they are dealt with.	Programs and initiatives are successfully implemented to prevent adverse effects occurring in the workplace. Leaders are proactively engaged in awareness building and advocacy for personal and process safety excellence.	The principle is integrated into every decision-making process to preemptively safeguard any harm from occurring to the workforce. Initiatives also include workers' mental health and social well-being. Executives' incentive plans are tied to this principle.	Communities the business serves, and the species that are affected by business operations are safeguarded from any harm that threatens their existences. A percentage of organizational profits are set aside for enhancing programs and initiatives dealing with this principle.

> **?** Before you go to the next chapter, I would like you to pause and ask yourself the following questions:

1 How is propensity to consume related to our **Preservation of Life** on this planet?

2 How is deforestation affecting the animals whose lives depend on it?

Chapter 6
The Second Principle: Preservation of Dignity

> We ought not to seek human welfare in ideas that are intrinsically dehumanizing or seek human happiness in a system that tries to quantify happiness.
>
> — **Caner Dagli,**
> Associate Professor at College of the Holy Cross

THE DESIRE FOR equality and eradication of prejudice regarding race, ethnicity, ancestry, socioeconomic status, gender, and disability are some good examples of what the **Preservation of Dignity** embodies. Every major world religion proclaims that human beings are fundamentally equal because the human race is one species. Judaism and Christianity espouse this inalienable right as a consequence of mankind's status as children of God. In Hinduism, it is a manifestation of the Divine. In Buddhism, equality is the common original nature and desire for enlightenment. In Islam, maintaining human equity is a moral and spiritual obligation of the community as a whole and also for each of its members. Faith-based traditions require a commitment to justice in order to create social harmony. The good of the whole and the good of the individual are not seen as competing interests. Each individual has the duty to uphold this moral standard, to dignify one another, and the community is collectively obliged to safeguard this tenent. Stemming from this collective obligation is the balancing act of rights and responsibilities; one cannot enjoy one without ensuring the other.

Preservation of Dignity, in the context of a free enterprise system, is the implicit requirement to safeguard the dignity of all stakeholders from predatory or exploitative practices. Any system, even if it is a free market system, is as strong as its weakest link. The long-term sustainability of free markets is built on the premise that entrepreneurship, ingenuity, trade, commerce, advancement, and prosperity are open to all who participate in the system.

But in order to maintain trust and fairness in participation, the weak (the workforce, vendors, suppliers, etc.) need their dignity safeguarded. On the other hand, the strong (the corporations and their owners, the banks, and Wall Street) need accountability in fulfilling their responsibilities. That is why we have checks and balances put in place: to maintain fairness in the system. Sometimes, this monitoring comes from regulatory agencies; and other times, it is self imposed by companies in the form of governance mechanisms or management systems. The aim, however, is to create impartiality to allow free markets to flourish and prosper; not at the expense of anyone, but for the greater good of the society at large.

Over the last 50 years, the buttresses keeping the US free enterprise system afloat have gradually eroded. The reason for this erosion has been the acute focus on wealth generation for a few at the top. This short-sightedness permeates the governance of our affairs in both public and private sectors, fueling a double standard for preserving the dignity of all its participants and exacerbating inequality.

As a result, when there is an economic downturn, the workforce takes the hit, the taxpayers pay the price, Corporate America gets bailed out, and the CEOs walk away without any consequences, even when they are guilty of negligence.

A case in point is Dennis Muilenburg, former CEO of Boeing, who walked away with around $60 million in pension benefits and stock after he was ousted for his handling of the 737 Max crisis that caused the deaths of over 300 people. Our criminal justice system, tax code, and labor laws—all key aspects of maintaining harmony within society—unjustly favor a select few at the expense of the many. In 2017, an *Iowa Law Review* study reported that the majority of federal judges in white-collar cases "frequently sentence well below the fraud guideline".[12] It is not a surprise then that so many of the top managers of established US institutes escape the criminal justice system. According to an article in the *Hill*, published in December 2016, none of the chief executives of the companies that caused the 2008 global financial crisis have been held fully accountable to date. Nobody from Lehman Brothers or Citigroup has been criminally charged. No top executives at Bear Stearns have been indicted. Not one of any of the top executives of the big mortgage companies involved—Washington Mutual, IndyMac and Countrywide—had to face the law. The biggest banks—JPMorgan, Bank of America, Citibank, Deutsche Bank and, more recently, Wells Fargo—were accused of fraud and contributing to financial decline not seen since the Great Depression, but none faced accountability,[13] highlighting a deficient emotional system, characterized by lethargy on part of the regulators.

The lower wage earners, middle class, and hourly wage earners (who have not seen significant wage increases for over 30 years) are considered mere cogs whose purpose in life is to churn the corporate machine. When the workforce is leveraged as merely an input in the production process, it translates into overhead that needs to be controlled and optimized. Human capital then becomes a variable in a business's optimization strategy, like any other material resource. With a push for extracting maximum benefits from the workforce, companies conveniently justify adjustments (i.e. right-sizing and downsizing) to rebalance their profit and loss equations.

An article recently published in *Marker-Medium*, entitled 'Companies Don't Need to Lay People Off to Survive', tells a very encouraging story of a CEO of a $3 billion company who saved all his 12,000 employees from layoffs. In the 2008 global financial crisis, 12 years ago, the world economy came to a standstill and thousands lost their jobs, while businesses went into liquidation. However, even under these circumstances, one organization did not lay off its employees and took a radically different approach to ensure its survival. The cost-cutting measures implemented by Barry-Wehmiller, a St. Louis-based manufacturing company, could serve as a good business model for the **Preservation of Dignity.**

Instead of laying off its employees, the board at Barry-Wehmiller suspended its executive bonuses and 401(k) plans. The CEO, Bob Chapman, reduced his own salary from $875,000 to $10,500 (which was his starting salary in 1968). Finally, the company asked all its employees to take four weeks of unpaid time off. The plan received an overwhelmingly positive response from all employees who were scared of losing their jobs. Implementing the unpaid time off policy was challenging, but it significantly boosted the team spirit. Employees traded their time off so those who were worse off did not have to bear the brunt of the recession. As a result of its unique strategy, the company was able to bounce back after the recession without losing any of its skilled employees, and 2010 became the best year of the company's history.[14] Bob's emotional, behavioral, and cognitive systems governing his character exhibited the kind of dynamic equilibrium that created justice and fairness in his action.

This principle celebrates the traits and practices of respect and dignity to all stakeholders, regardless of their role or function. In this global age of supply chain systems, if the collective well-being and welfare of all stakeholders are sidelined or ignored, the lowest wage earners suffer the greatest inequities as corporate inequality is propagated. According to Oxfam, farmers and workers who grow and process food are often left without enough to eat themselves. The major cause of this supply chain inequity stems from the supermarkets. Their business model is based on intense competition with each other. As a result, they squeeze their suppliers for the best margins possible. Winnie Byanyima, the Executive Director of Oxfam International, states: "What chance does a poor woman food producer at the other end of the global trade have in the face of a trillion-dollar buying sector? ...she has to peel up to 950 shrimps an hour to receive her minimum wage. She avoids going to the toilet and stands for nine hours at a time. It would take her more than 5,000 years to make the average annual salary of a top supermarket CEO in the US".[15] How much of that pain and suffering does the C-suite feel any given day?

Willis Towers Watson's 2020 Workplace Dignity Survey of over 40,000 employees across 27 markets, including 8,000 employees in the US, reveals that workplace dignity is a key part of a healthy work environment. Employers are beginning to see how a healthier workforce lowers healthcare costs while contributing to greater productivity and performance. Low levels of stress improve people's attitudes and willingness to contribute above and beyond what is expected of them.

According to the survey, 80% of senior executives believe that a culture of dignity promotes self-respect, pride, and self-worth. Conversely, only 65% of these companies' employees felt they were treated with respect and dignity.

Creating a culture of dignity is a multi-layered endeavor. Employers may be content to provide a work environment free of discrimination, harassment, exclusion, and bullying. Although this may classify as 'dignity at work', two other layers are missing, according to the survey. The first is employee satisfaction, which can be defined as recognition for their contributions to something meaningful. The second is employee respect. Employees being paid wages to sustain a good standard of living, and sufficient health benefits that will not cause bankruptcy to themselves and their dependents in times of emergency, contributes to employee respect. That extends to equal pay for women as well.

The survey also points out that 86% of employers believe senior organizational leaders have a sincere interest in their employees' well-being and 65% believe they make it possible for employees to have a healthy work-life balance. However, in both instances, only 50% of employees agreed with those statements.[16] A gaping 36% differential was unaccounted for.

Businesses are organic matter, made up of people. By their very nature, they are social entities that require diversity of opinion and thought to create growth strategy, and uniqueness of talent and skill to create ingenuity, capabilities, and competencies. Diversity only happens when others are given the dignity to participate and have a seat at the table. Recognition and understanding of diversity and equality, and how these concepts can be applied in uplifting the human spirit, is essential for the provision of dignity in engagement with all stakeholders. A preservation-centered approach can support dignity in the workplace, acknowledging and valuing each person's diversity. An article on diversity published by Forbes in 2018 references a study by Boston Consulting Group (BCG), which found that increasing the diversity of leadership teams leads to better innovation and improved financial performance. In the study, BCG looked at 1,700 different companies across eight countries, with varying industries and company sizes. They found that increasing diversity had a direct effect on the bottomline. Companies that had more diverse management teams had 19% higher revenues due to innovation.[17]

Preservation of Dignity is tied to the commitment of inclusivity and equity in the workplace. This principle stands, on one hand, as a deterrent to unjust exercises of power. It curbs the potential for violation of workers' rights in its practitioners. Disregard of this principle is evident in cases where factory workers are exposed to hazardous working conditions without adequate safety equipment. Or when a community's drinking water supply is polluted due to chemical effluents from production processes. Or the monumental environmental and social harm created by the overuse of single-use plastics globally. On the other hand, this principle is an enabler for the eradication of the workforce gender wage gap, hiring biases, discriminating on the basis of sexual orientation, racially motivated discriminatory practices in serving customers, and so on and so forth.

In July 2018, *Inc* magazine published an article on how Mark Benioff, the CEO of Salesforce, a San Francisco-based cloud computing company that sells customer relationship management tools, closed a six million dollar compensation gap affecting gender, race, and ethnicity across the company. The CEO also mandated the presence of at least 30% of women at all leadership meetings to facilitate the promotion of women leaders. It is Benioff's progressive leadership that has made Salesforce a strong equality advocate for its own workforce and the communities it serves in.[18]

Table 5 offers a simple maturity assessment guide to evaluate your organization's current state of **Preservation of Dignity**. It serves as a good starting point to quickly determine the critical success factors needed to implement this at your organization. As you go through the assessment, I would like you to keep the following two questions in mind:

1. What are the accelerators and drivers for this principle at your organization?

2. Determine where your organization is on this chart. Then ask your self: what are the inhibitors, challenges, and pitfalls that prevent advancement to the next stage?

Table 5: Preservation of Dignity - Maturity Assessment

Stage 0 Subpar	Stage 1 Reactive	Stage 2 Developing	Stage 3 Advance	Stage 4 Leading
Preservation of Dignity is not a critical component of the business philosophy. Annual surveys are conducted to measure employee engagement and supervisors go through mandatory HR training in personnel management, only focused on discrimination and harassment.	Programs and initiatives are in place, highlighting the commitment to inclusivity and equity. Fair compensation is talked about, which includes supply chain stakeholders, but implementation is not complete.	A human capital strategy of building a culture of dignity is implemented. There is leadership support and accountability, with targeted training and communication. Program metrics are in place to monitor progress to enhance performance.	Dignity for all is a core aspect of how business is conducted. There is active leadership in promoting a culture of dignity. Priorities and strategies put in place are now showing qualitative and quantitative results, such as pay programs that are fair, transparent, and performance-based.	Preservation of Dignity is fully integrated in the DNA of the culture that extends well into the supply chain. A culture of well-being, that addresses the need of the whole person through a focus on the physical, financial, emotional and social aspects, is evident in all aspects of the business.

? Before you go to the next chapter, I would like you to pause and ask yourself the following questions:

1 When was the last time you, as the leader, were in the trenches with your team to experience first-hand the working conditions, atmosphere, and emotional health of your workforce?

2 What are you doing to create interpersonal trust amongst your team to improve the organization's functions so that goals and objectives can be achieved?

Chapter 7
The Third Principle: The Preservation of Reason

> Reason is the source of knowledge, the place where it first manifests itself, and the foundation upon which it stands.
>
> — Al-Ghazali,
> 11th century Sufi mystic

A FEW YEARS ago, a manufacturing client retained my team to assess the maturity of their corporate environmental health and safety (EHS) programs, and the culture around safety. Actively growing their enterprise, acquisitions were high on their agenda, and a potential buyout transaction was imminent. Their board needed to understand management's ability to handle various scenarios after the merger concerning the expanded footprint of their operation. Some of the areas to be addressed included operational performance, scalability of the EHS programs, and their impact on the organizational culture.

As our team's assessment phase came to an end, the client's lack of understanding of the 'current' state of the EHS programs, which were not scalable, was very apparent. The Director of EHS reported to the Vice President of Operations (VP) and was the only person who comprehended the risk of not upgrading the programs and upskilling his team accordingly.

Given his reporting structure, he felt constrained in his ability to persuade his boss to see the safety risk at hand. The director had been in a similar situation with a different company in the past. He had witnessed a serious accident and knew that an increase in the operational footprint meant more assets to manage, and this would further exacerbate his team's ability to manage personnel and asset safety.

In his mind, the only option to mitigate the risks were to update the EHS programs, retrain the workforce, and enhance the organizational culture. The operations budget was tight, as the company was in a transactional phase. His repeated attempts at asking for additional funding fell on deaf ears. The VP was in favor of barreling through to expand his team's operational footprint.

The director was on the agenda for a debrief at an upcoming board meeting. Two days before that meeting, I received a frantic call from him hoping for a Hail Mary. He requested that I help the VP see the big picture.

I had just finished reading the *Alchemy of Happiness* by Al-Ghazali. It featured his original model of the human psyche, as previously discussed in this book (emotional, behavioral, and cognitive). I had an "Aha!" moment. I understood that the ability to reason emanated from a mindset where the emotional, behavioral, and cognitive systems all worked in sync and were centered.

A rational mind can best anticipate the consequences of future decisions in a state of equilibrium. I discovered it could also calculate in advance the results of actions taken. With that in mind, I realized that temperamental choices are, therefore, devoid of courage or wisdom. Based on these insights, I had two tasks at hand:

1. Ascertain the intention behind the decision-making process for both parties.

2. Get them to verbalize the desired outcome they were trying to achieve.

After speaking at length with both of them, it became obvious that the VP's priority was to fuel financial growth to increase his profit-sharing in the short term. His 'me' thinking mentality seemed to exemplify an emotional excessiveness that potentially manifested as gluttony and greed.

He exhibited a behavioral deficiency, which was displayed by his indifference and complacency of the safety risks by overloading the EHS team. In his short time in production, he had never experienced a serious accident. Consequently, he lacked the hindsight to make an objective evaluation. On the other hand, the director, who had experienced the devastating effects of stretching teams beyond their capacity, was extremely apprehensive and could not barrel through with the plan.

The above example shows that when a person or institution does not take the time to fully examine issues, problems, and their underlying causes, they can easily fall into the category of negligence. The VP's lopsided and hurried rationale downplayed the potential risks of expansion. His subconscious was most likely in denial, so he pushed away what he perceived could be a 'negative' outcome.

The question still remains unanswered: how to resolve the scalability issue and get acknowledgement that the risk would outweigh any rewards?

The VP made his decision based upon the logic of putting his perceived interests and objectives first: profitability over safety, a type of confirmation bias, where he looked at what confirmed his beliefs and ignored what contradicted them.

A person's decision-making process goes through a sequence of cognitive steps. It starts with the establishment of objectives or goals in a contextual framework. Multiple variables such as the origin of information and confirmation biases are then filtered through. Past experiences and beliefs further motivates our rationality, emotionally influencing our decisions. As a result, we may downplay and at times overlook the reality on the ground.

Luckily, at the last minute, the board meeting got pushed out a month, giving us extra time with the VP. We had a few additional sessions with him, where we were able to provide him with an enriched context to articulate the value of keeping his production lines up and running. We had shared stories of safety-near-misses that could potentially have life-changing impacts for his team. Lastly, we gathered industry opinions from his peers on best-in-class safety operational risk management.

His "Aha!" moment eventually came. I came to know of this while waiting for a call from the director to explore other data to convince the VP of our mission. When my phone rang, it was the VP instead. After thanking me for my efforts to transform his opinion, he was ready to talk to the board about the need to upgrade all existing EHS programs. Surprised at what I was hearing, I asked him what made him change his mind?

He told me that for five years, twice a week, he had been giving his wife a ride to work. He was always first in the truck waiting for her with the engine running. Because he was constantly in a rush, he would put the truck in reverse, release the hand-break and put his foot on the brake-paddle the moment he saw her coming out of the house.

That morning, his wife walked briskly towards the truck from the back of the vehicle. His foot accidentally hit the accelerator instead of the brake. The truck moved back about a foot before he was able to stop it, but it was too late. His wife flew a couple of feet in the air and landed on her side. Other than a few bruises, she was fortunately unharmed.

But the VP's sense of reasoning underwent a jolt that day. All he kept thinking of was how badly he could have hurt, or worse, killed her. That nanosecond was enough to recalibrate his thought process and relate that situation to his work issues. He had taken the day off after the incident. He later shared with me the thought running through his mind on that near-fatal day: "What was I thinking?"

Years later, I checked in with him to talk about organizational improvements. He boasted that his company doubled in size, production numbers had never been better, and his team had never been so in tune with personal and process safety management.

In another example, we are witnessing the US government's response to COVID-19 play out in real time. The federal administration's focus, from the start, had been on the national economy, instead of the safety of the citizens. When our elected officials, who are supposed to be public servants, are more interested in holding on to power than serving the citizenry, the logic that drives their decisions is acutely focused on short-term gains (the upcoming elections, in this case). Because our politics is so intertwined with capitalism, a politician's electability is defined by how well the economy is doing, not the well-being of the people. As a result, in spite of having world-class infectious disease experts, medical technology, and emergency response capabilities, and even with ample time to prepare, our government has yet to come up with a coherent strategy for containment. Thousands of US citizens have needlessly lost their lives due to a lack of unified strategy and consistency of messaging around prevention and safeguard measures. **The Preservation of Reason** is not seemingly in play in this example.

Such behaviors bely people and institutions that have not learned to confront reality in a rational or systematic way. It is difficult for people of this persuasion to see the big picture in such situations. Instead, they stay focused on the immediate gains.

When practiced sincerely, the **Preservation of Reason** acts as a coach to guide and fortify our intentions through the decision-making process in alignment with the four other principles: **life, dignity, wealth**, and the **future**. Once this process is internalized and embedded in the psyche of the decision-maker, then thoughts void of these principles are rejected at the subconscious level. With time and practice, cognitive dissonance is reduced when deciding between self interest and the greater good. This strengthening of the decision-maker's resolve to do the right thing brings a sense of overall confidence and contentment. In **MBI** terminology, that would be promoting good and preventing harm.

Other very real and seldom acknowledged aspects which impedes our ability to make sound decisions is the amount of information which is available to us instantly, and even to a level of overload. We are bombarded by information 24/7 via social media, TV, podcasts, emails, etc. Sifting through large amounts of information, even before determining its applicability or context, can become an overbearing feat. Many organizations address this issue with technology; by packaging information into data points, charts, graphs, models, and summaries which are compiled and rolled up for leadership to base their decisions on. But does leadership acknowledge the rationale on which the information was synthesized, or the experiences that influenced the individuals who distilled the information?

Leaders are seldom aware of their own biases, let alone the biases of their teams. Rationality in decision-making cannot be invoked without prejudice, if the contextual references of the decision-maker are skewed because of real or perceived pressures. Consulting companies are notorious in this regard. They preach what they infrequently practice. How talent is acquired, leveraged, and then, disposed of, is predominantly centered around financial profitability. Decisions to hire or fire are typically driven by operational greed, like that of the VP of operations in the earlier example. Being in the consulting field all my life, I have first-hand experience of inapt operational leads only relying on spreadsheets to drive their sector growth strategies. Most get there by default, and many have no understanding of their organization's vision, mission, or the ethical approach to business growth.

We see the same logic in many large enterprises, manifested from a different perspective. As more demands are placed on the C-suite teams to make decisions, and make them fast, an increasing number of leaders offload the responsibilities of distilling information to other levels, with the assumption that the assigned teams or individuals have the required experiences, rationale, or holistic view of the organization. Decisions cannot be only about hard data crunching and analytics, where numbers are easy to manipulate, when all you have are data points in front of you.

We saw this type of a disconnect in rationale in the case of Volkswagen. It took an emissions scandal, which cost them over $20 billion in fines, to embrace the new 'goTOzero' environmental mission statement.

In a press statement in July 2019, Oliver Blume, Member of the Group Board of Management responsible for environmental protection, said: "With the new Group Environmental Policy, the group and its stakeholders have a clear orientation. Our efforts to improve environmental protection cover the entire product cycle, from development, production, and operation to the subsequent recycling of our vehicles and administration. We will also involve our suppliers. Only together can we achieve our goals."[19]

What sense of reasoning did the Volkswagen leadership tap into when they allowed doctored emission data to be submitted to environmental regulators?

When making decisions devoid of the principles of **life**, **dignity**, **wealth**, and **future**, decision-makers forfeit intellectual vigor and dilute their capability to **reason**. Because Volkswagen's leadership only looked at data and numbers, which focused solely on accelerating growth, they took their eyes off the bigger picture. It is sad that an iconic global brand such as Volkswagen, known for its precision engineering and process excellence, would put their reputation and credibility on the line for short-term financial gains. At the time, when the news first came out, it seemed so unreasonable as to how and why Volkswagen would sacrifice their global reputation for short-term gains.

MBI-centric decision-making takes into account the understanding of people, their rationality, emotions, and behavior along with data-centric information. It creates an environment of sound rationality and judgment, whereby leaders are willing to walk away from self-interest (i.e. profits, individual gains, prestige, power, etc.) to preserve **life**, **dignity**, **wealth**, and the **future** of and for all their stakeholders.

Table 6 offers a maturity assessment guide to evaluate your organization's current stance on the **Preservation of Reason**. It serves as a good starting point to quickly determine the critical success factors needed for implementation. As you go through the assessment, I would like you to keep the following two questions in mind:

1. What are the accelerators and drivers for this principle at your organization?

2. Determine where your organization is on this chart. Then ask yourself: what are the inhibitors, challenges, and pitfalls that prevent advancement to the next stage?

Table 6: Preservation of Reason - Maturity Assessment

Stage 0 Subpar	Stage 1 Reactive	Stage 2 Developing	Stage 3 Advance	Stage 4 Leading
Preservation of Reason is not a critical component of the business philosophy. Hard data, analytics, and number crunching drive decisions.	A code of conduct, including rules, beliefs, values, and expectations is in place for compliance purposes. Decision-making is ad hoc, handled as a one-off with no alignment with long term strategic goals.	The executive leadership proactively participates in the decision-making process to evaluate all critical business risks and opportunities consistently. Simulation modeling, participatory planning, and decision analysis tools form the basis of their decision-making strategy.	Decision-making rights are both data-driven and data-informed. Business Intelligence (BI) systems are leveraged to optimize decision-making effectiveness. Biases are openly challenged and dissent is respected and encouraged to facilitate consensus and engagement at the levels of the organization.	Leadership competency requires understanding and application of universal principles of harm, justice, fairness, and care. Leadership behavior is evaluated and incentivized based on the impact they create in preserving life, dignity, reason, wealth, and future.

? Before you go to the next chapter, I would like you to pause and ask yourself the following questions:

1 How are your biases influencing your decision making? Especially, under stress?

2 When there is a tension between what is good for the individual and what is good for society, how do you bring those conflicting objectives into alignment, especially when critical information about the situation is missing?

Chapter 8
The Fourth Principle: Preservation of Wealth

> You cannot have the benefits of capitalist market growth without the support of a significant proportion, and indeed, virtually all of the people; and if you have an increasing sense that the rewards of capitalism are being distributed unjustly the system will not stand.
>
> — **Alan Greenspan,**
> former Chair of the Federal Reserve

ONCE THE PREVIOUS **MBI** practices have been put into motion—respecting lives and dignity; and applying reason and rationality to thought—the fourth principle kicks in.

The Preservation of Wealth principle is centered around holistic financial wellness for the organization and its workforce, first and foremost. This principle goes beyond the fiduciary responsibility of the board, for managing the wealth of shareholders alone. It also encompasses financial wellness for all stakeholders and, in particular, low-and moderate-income members. The essence of this principle is about the circulation of wealth in society after it has been earned by fair means.

Uncirculated wealth is akin to still water, which stagnates quickly and becomes a breeding ground for bacteria and viruses. Mosquitoes take advantage of still water and lay their larvae in it. These mosquitoes then are highly likely to transmit diseases, such as malaria and dengue to humans. Then, still water becomes a source of facilitating health crises for many of the world's vulnerable populations. Similarly, wealth that is hoarded and amassed in one place alone, benefits only a few, while depriving many who may have even contributed to its accumulation. A deprivation which results in the onset of many physical, social and psychological ailments; seeping into the many lives of the workforce, wreaking havoc in society. **The Preservation of Wealth**, therefore, becomes a call to rethink the current income distribution, corporate taxation, and cost externalization practices to facilitate a more fair and equitable distribution system.

It is not that there is a shortage of wealth in the system; unfortunately, over the last 50 years, the hyper-capitalist free enterprise system has witnessed a warped wealth circulation pattern. When the economy soars, and businesses turn healthy profits, corporate elites and Wall Street speculators earn heftily. But while productivity has grown exponentially, wages of the workforce have been more or less stagnant. This concept, where a few control the financial viability of the many, is not new to humanity. Examples are littered throughout history of manifestations of this type of unfair wealth distribution practiced by the elites of society. Whether it is the slave-landowner relationship, the subject-ruler dynamics of autocracies, or today's employee-employer model, they all exhibit similar patterns where the finances of the masses are tied to a few. They follow the same methodology of indentured service, where a few accumulate wealth on the backs of the many. As a result, the rich get richer, and the poor poorer.

It is no secret that, since 1978, CEO pay has grown about 100%, while worker compensation rose a measly 12%. The exorbitantly high senior management pay scales create a class system which intrinsically values management over the rest of the workforce. In fact, it extracts money from the cash coffers that should be paid to employees at the middle and bottom of the wage distribution. It is this imbalance that creates the '1% versus the 99%' mindset in almost all mid-to-large size corporations. This mindset is the core indicator of the indentured service methodology. It restricts wealth from trickling down to all members of the organization.

An example of systemic indentured service is the interest-only component of the mortgage system. The system in itself, works: the lender earns through funding the contract; and the recipient earns through access to ownership and appreciation of the asset. But the creative interest-only options that banks offer to lure in customers, who may not be able to afford a regular mortgage, entraps the customer in paying interest perpetually, without paying anything towards the principle, and therefore, never achieving "the ownership" they initially sought.

According to the Economic Policy Institute, the average annual pay for CEOs at the 350 largest firms was $18.9 million in 2017. But the pay of the next four highest-paid executives at these same firms totaled on average roughly the same amount as well. Given these numbers, it is hard to imagine that the next

10-20 highest-paid people in each of these companies are getting far less than one million dollars a year.

According to a 2020 study by the United Way ALICE Project, a staggering 40% of US households did not earn enough income for basic life necessities such as housing, health, food, shelter, or childcare.[20] This is yet another sad example of anemic wealth distribution practices, where the indentured classes cannot meet their basic needs of shelter, clothing, food, health, or education.

We see how this inequity in pay impacts employees, where most US households are now two-income families, often with two and even three jobs per person, and their household debt is increasing at alarming rates. With COVID-19 raging through communities, uncontained, many of these households will unfortunately soon become no-income families.

Imagine a scenario where the CEOs of large companies are making two to three million dollars per year instead. If that were the case, then the next four highest-paid executives at each company would probably be paid close to one million dollars each. The senior management would probably be in the $400,000 to $800,000 range. Over the longer run, some of the savings in executive pay could be passed along to frontline workers in the form of higher wages.

A great CEO-to-worker pay ratio rebalancing act is Seattle-based Gravity Payments' CEO Dan Price. In 2015, Price decided to increase his employees' pay after he read a study on happiness. Based on the study, there was strong correlation between making $75,000 annually and a person's emotional well-being. He made the decision to increase the salaries for his 120 employees in Seattle, raising the minimum salary to $70,000. He reduced his one-million-dollar salary by 90% in order to make this happen.[21] Here is what that rebalancing did for his workforce:

1. It doubled the pay of about 30 workers and gave an additional 40 significant raises.
2. The higher wages transformed the lives of his employees; more than 10% purchased a house for the first time.
3. Individual 401(k) contributions more than doubled.

The systemic effect of income inequality forces management to pay more attention to operational strategies that promote leveraging tax loopholes and creative cost externalization maneuvers. All such strategies lead to the curtailment of money flow to the workforce. As a result, costs are externalized, and the burden gets shifted to society at large.

Look at any industry sector, and you will find egregious violations of the cost externalization practice. How many corporations have benefited from R&D paid for by the public's tax dollars? Did the tech giants who leverage online spaces as their sole revenue-generating model invent the internet? Obviously not! Many US corporations not only exclusively profit from these 'public' investments, but they do not pay taxes that would then benefit the public. Originally, this was the reason for public investment in private enterprise, to gain from the increased taxes it would create. Instead, many of these corporations avoid the concept of corporate taxation.

In 2019, the combined revenue of just two such tech giants, Amazon and Netflix, was over $300 billion. Amazon has been around for decades, but only paid its first round of income taxes in 2016. According to SEC filings, the total taxes paid by Amazon for 2019 was $162 million. That is a tax rate of a meagre 1.2%. Netflix did not pay any taxes for 2019. A recent report by *Fortune* on Amazon, Apple, Facebook, Google, Microsoft, and Netflix—nicknamed the 'Silicon Six' by the non-profit Fair Tax Mark—claims a major gap in the taxes they might be expected to owe, and how much they actually pay. According to the report, between 2010 and 2019, using legal tax avoidance strategies that have become popular among corporations, the taxes paid collectively by the companies across all global territories in which they operate was $155.3 billion less than what the actual tax rates would have required. When considering not only the cash paid, but money put aside for future taxes, the gap was still $100.2 billion.[22] When global corporations escape taxation, the adverse effects are localized, impacting the public social safety-nets the communities depend upon, such as necessary public services.

Americans for Tax Fairness (ATF), a collective of more than 420 national, state and local organizations united in support of a fair tax system, reports,

"US corporations dodge $90 billion a year in income taxes by shifting profits to subsidiaries—often no more than post office box—in tax havens". Not to mention many do not pay taxes altogether. Only 55 Fortune 500 companies disclose what they would expect to pay in US taxes if these profits were not officially booked offshore. All told, these 55 companies would collectively owe $147.5 billion in additional federal taxes. To put this enormous sum in context, it represents more than the entire state budgets of California, Virginia, and Indiana combined.[23] Imagine the greater good that can be achieved by the public sector collecting the fair share of these companies' taxes. That money is needed to uplift the masses with better education, living conditions and health care; all are major sources of contention between the haves and have nots.

Cost externalization also includes bailouts and subsidies. According to Deborah J. Lucas, MIT Sloan professor of finance and director of the MIT Golub Center for Finance and Policy, the total direct cost of crisis-related bailouts (2008-2009) on a fair value basis was about $498 billion, which amounted to over 3% of the GDP in 2009. As for who directly benefited, Lucas found that the main winners were the large, unsecured creditors of large financial institutions. While their exact identities have not been made public, most are likely to have been large institutional investors such as banks, insurance companies, sovereigns, pension and mutual funds.[24]

Fast forward to 2020, as the COVID-19 pandemic rages on, it is the airline industry being bailed out. The industry grew at a compound annual rate of approximately 6% over the last decade, hitting over $800 billion in revenue in 2019 over the previous year. Leaving aside loans, the industry received $25 billion in grants to pay workers through September 2020. The industry has made billions in profits over the last decade. Where did all that money go?

It turns out that US airlines spend over 90% of their cash on stock buybacks to enrich their investors and executives, making them wealthier than ever. It is this push from activist investors that, when coupled with executive greed, creates a culture within the industry where a mere 2% of their revenues is deemed acceptable as cash balance. It does not take an accountant to figure out that these clearly reflect cost externalization practices that benefit the few at the expense of the many.

It stands to reason that if capitalism is indeed a real free enterprise system, one that is open for trade and commerce to all, then everyone in that system should benefit from it equal to the amount of effort they have put it. Yet that has not been the case for decades now. The CEO of Amazon, Jeff Bezos, makes approximately $2,500 per second! When money is syphoned to the top, bypassing critical stakeholders, the system experiences gross inequities. As a result, there is an imbalance of wealth and influence that is creating abuse of privilege and power.

This 'rigged' system of distribution, which entails both circulation and reinvestment of wealth as it now stands, is having catastrophic effects on our society. History shows that too much concentration of wealth at the top, and stagnation everywhere else, indicates a system nearing collapse.

How can we bring back balance to a system where many are rewarded for following its current imbalanced principles?

A great story of the equitable distribution of wealth is Chobani, the Greek yogurt maker. In 2016, founder, CEO and immigrant Hamdi Ulukaya granted his entire staff of 2,000 employees shares in the company worth up to 10%.

In a letter to his employees, he stated that the shares were not 'gifts', but a mutual promise to work together with a shared sense of purpose and responsibility. His goal was to continue to create something unique and of lasting value with the entire staff.

The deal gave all employees an average stake of $150,000 in the $3 billion company.[25] If Chobani goes public, some of its employees could potentially become millionaires. But employee ownership is not the only purposeful act Hamdi initiated. He consistently hired refugees; a practice he believes not only helps build his business, but also improves the entire community because of the diversity of culture, thoughts, and perspectives.

It is easy to imagine the team's level of commitment to creating something unique and long-lasting. More CEOs need to pick up Hamdi's playbook and run with it.

Out of all the preservation principles, this one is the most difficult to implement, since it infringes on decades-old practices infused with privileges. Once privilege gets firmly infused in our psyche, it creates a sense of entitlement that breeds indifference to the pain and suffering of others.

I remember watching a TEDx talk by Paul Piff, Assistant Professor of Psychology and Social Behavior at the University of California, who argued that as people become affluent, they tend to feel less compassionate and empathetic towards others, and their sense of entitlement increases. He talked about the Monopoly experiment he ran with over 100 students, who were made to flip a coin to determine whether they would be poor or privileged. The privileged players received more cash, collected twice as much money as they passed 'Go', and were permitted to roll the dice twice. He noticed that the wealthier players became increasingly condescending towards their less fortunate counterparts, and less sensitive to their plight. The rich players were demonstrative of their material success.

Outside of this experiment, looking at the examples I have used, we see the same formula at play, where corporate executives who earn in the millions are completely disconnected with the frontline employees, who barely earn minimum wage, and therefore need multiple jobs to secure basic necessities to lead a decent life.

Preservation of Wealth does not suggest giving all your wealth away. It merely reinforces the fact that no leader builds an organization alone. While it is necessary for a leader to have the vision and wisdom to chart the course, it is the workforce, the labor, that puts in the muscle to make things happen. Organizational leaders must figure out a way to level the playing field for their respective teams; as Hamdi, Price, and many other conscience-driven leaders are doing.

Table 7 offers a simple maturity assessment guide to evaluate your organization's current **Preservation of Wealth** system. It serves as a good starting point to quickly determine the critical success factors needed to implement this principle at your organization. As you go through the assessment, I would like you to keep the following questions in mind:

1. What are the accelerators and drivers for this principle at your organization?

2. Determine where your organization is on this chart. Then ask yourself: what are the inhibitors, challenges, and pitfalls that prevent advancement to the next stage?

Table 7: Preservation of Wealth - Maturity Assessment

Stage 0 Subpar	Stage 1 Reactive	Stage 2 Developing	Stage 3 Advance	Stage 4 Leading
Primary focus is on wealth accumulation by any means possible for the shareholders.	Accumulation of wealth is tied to products and services that benefit society, but may not be sustainable in the long run as they potentially pose harm to the environment.	Accumulation of wealth is tied to products and services that benefit society.	Wealth is created through innovative and impactful means; tied to solving broader challenges in business and society.	Wealth creation is aligned with the notion of protecting the planet, with products and services that service public interest.
Management team is rewarded for reaching their profitability targets.		Concerted effort is made to curtail cost externalization practices.	All external costs are assigned and quantified.	Management sacrifices profit margins to support workforce and community upliftment.
Costs externalization and tax loopholes are a critical component of corporate growth.	Employee benefits, some profit-sharing for middle tier management, and charitable giving are structured programs which support policies of wealth redistribution.	Organization is committed to redistributing wealth to all stakeholders equitably in the form of higher wages, profit sharing, and community partnerships.	Wealth is shared equitably between all stakeholders. CEO-to-worker pay ratios, gender pay parity, and equitable tax policies are critical components of the strategy.	The business pays its full share of taxes equitably; without taking undue advantage of any offshore tax sheltering.

? Before you go to the next chapter, I would like you to pause and ask yourself the following questions:

1 What would it take to convert some or all your stakeholders into shareholders?

2 Employees are asked to sacrifice benefits, pay, holidays and sometimes their jobs when an organization is in a downturn. What are you willing to sacrifice as a leader?

Chapter 9
The Fifth Principle: Preservation of the Future

> We are leaving a terrible legacy of poisoning and diminishment of the environment for our grandchildren's grandchildren, generations not yet born. Some people have called that intergeneration[al] tyranny, a form of taxation without representation, levied by us on generations yet to be. It's the wrong thing to do.
>
> — **Ray Anderson,**
> Founder & CEO Interface

ACCORDING TO THE World Economic Forum's *Global Risks Report 2020*, the last five years are the warmest on record. Natural disasters are becoming more intense and frequent. The previous year witnessed unprecedented and extreme weather patterns throughout the world. Alarmingly, global temperatures are on track to increase by at least 3°C towards the end of the century; twice the figure climate experts had warned is the limit to avoid the most severe economic, social and environmental consequences.[26] For the first time in the 15 year history of the report, environmental risks—extreme weather, climate action failure, natural disasters, and biodiversity loss—take up the top five spots for long-term risks to our planet by likelihood of occurrence and impact.

There is a direct correlation between these environmental crises and the resulting economic, social, and political turmoil. The fact that we are losing heavily on mission critical issues such as environmental stewardship and climate change, social equity and justice, and income and wealth parity, puts pressure on businesses to take the lead in addressing the world's woes. The fifth and last principle of **MBI**, therefore, is the **Preservation of the Future**. It is about the thoughtful and strategic stewardship of our planet.

As caring and responsible stewards of the earth, we cannot ignore or normalize behavior that degrades the environment, depletes natural resources, pollutes the waterways and destroys the natural habitats of species, knowing that such actions have detrimental impacts on humanity, especially the future generations. The loss of biodiversity alone is having a direct impact on human health since ecosystems are no longer adequate to meet social needs. Alterations in biodiversity changes the ecosystem which consequently affects livelihoods, income, local migration and, on occasion, may even cause geopolitical conflict.

The *Guardian* published a report in October 2018 with research showing that since 1970, humanity has wiped out 60% of other mammals, birds, fish, and reptiles. Experts now say that the annihilation of wildlife at these rates poses serious threats to our civilization. Zoologists and disease experts tell us that when animals are stressed, they shed parasites and viruses that, in an otherwise healthy state, are integrated into their bodies. In a National Institute of Health (NIH) study published in January 2019, it appeared that many coronaviruses had origins in a variety of bat species. With next generation sequencing technology and the increased surveillance of wild animal species, a large number of novel coronaviruses have already been identified. The NIH study claims that over 200 novel coronaviruses have been identified in bats. Like many other animal species, bats are now apparently existing in a heightened state of stress, as they are hunted or driven out of their natural habitats. Scientists are identifying how increased stress causes wildlife to excrete the coronavirus from their systems, which is harmless in their original hosts, but wreaks havoc when shed onto other beings. When frazzled bats get in close proximity to other mammals, such as human beings, the virus 'jumps' to the new hosts. In the scientific world, this is known as zoonotic spillover.

In a CNN interview, Dr Andrew Cunningham, Professor of Wildlife Epidemiology at the Zoological Society of London said, "The underlying causes of zoonotic spillover from bats or from other wild species have almost—always—been shown to be human behavior".[27]

This spillover is nothing new, but in the past, if humans were the recipients of a spillover virus and lived in a remote place, by the time they reached a larger population, they would have either overcome the infection, or died fighting it. The spillover would end, and the case closed. Thanks to rapid globalization, and humans jetting around the world before they even realize that they have been affected or infected, the rate of exposure to such spills and resulting transmissions has increased exponentially. Zoonotic spillover is on the forefront of preserving human life and is rapidly becoming global business continuity risk. It should be chalked up on the ever-growing list of dangerous practices of human beings.

Fueled by decades of hyper-capitalism, man-made environmental disasters are exponentially growing as well. Global enterprises have elected to pass down the cost of their pollution, their wastefulness and the destruction of natural resources onto future generations (i.e. cost externalization). While this may be considered standard operating behavior to achieve economic growth, and its side effects thought to be negligible, we are now experiencing the impact at the cellular levels.

About a decade ago, I took a sustainability course, where the instructor shared a slide that listed over a hundred chemicals. A small font was used to fit all the chemical names onto one page. She asked us if we knew where the sample was taken from. Looking at the types of chemicals listed, the majority of the class thought it was contaminated soil; it was a sustainability course after all. Some thought it came from a polluted river; others were convinced it was a sample from a toxic waste disposal facility.

We were all wrong.

To our shock, the instructor revealed that it was a sample of breast milk. She further explained that not all mothers' milk has that much contamination, but that there are numerous places in the world, including in the US, where this sample would be applicable. According to a New York Times article published on June 1, 2017, a pregnant woman's placenta reveals a shocking amount of toxins. Analysis of biomonitoring data from the Centers for Disease Control and Prevention found 59 toxic chemicals, pollutants and metals in expecting mothers, many of which were also found in the umbilical cord of newborns (77 maternal and 65 paired umbilical cord blood samples collected in San Francisco during 2010-2011). These chemicals and contaminants are part of our lives: they are in our food supplies, utensils, fabrics, clothing, furniture that contains flame retardants, and in the air we breathe in the form of combustion-related air pollutants from fossil-fuel-burning power plants and vehicles.[28]

The younger generation is particularly vulnerable. The World Health Organization estimates that children younger than five bear more than 40% of the global burden of disease caused by environmental risk factors, and 88% of the disease burden caused by climate change. A notable increase in the developmental problems seen in children worldwide has paralleled the proliferation of synthetic chemicals in our air, water, food, and consumer products. It is now estimated that one in six children in the US is affected by a developmental disability. These are complex disorders with multiple causes—genetic, social and environmental—often interacting with one another to increase the overall health and well-being risk for children across this planet.[29]

In the systems of the natural world, zero waste is produced. The output of one system becomes the input for another; this is also done in a very symbiotic manner. When living organisms die and decay, they are converted into nutrients for the soil. The soil feeds the vegetation that grows from it. The vegetation, in turn, becomes a source of nutrition and fuel for all types of life forms on the planet, including human beings. In comparison, man-made systems are not designed for perpetuity; they are often flawed and produce outputs which are not useful for any other system, therefore classified as waste.

Consider a one liter plastic water bottle, made out of polyethylene terephthalate (PET), a resin derived from petroleum and natural gas. These fossil fuels are heated up and mixed with water to create plastic. A typical one-liter plastic bottle uses about two liters of water during its manufacturing process. One-liter bottle of water represents three liters of water consumption. Each of those bottles takes about four million joules of energy to create. Every ton of this plastic that is produced creates three tons of carbon dioxide. Between manufacturing and transportation, about 63 billion gallons of fuel is used to supply bottled water nationally, every year. The majority of these bottles are discarded after just one use, and 91% of plastic does not actually end up getting recycled.

Takes 3 Bottles of Water to Produce 1	1 Ton of Plastic Creates	Energy to Produce 1 Bottle	Fuel Used per Year to Supply Water	Bottles Not Recycled
3L = 1L	3T CO_2	4M J	63B Gal	91%

According to the EPA, the average American produces about 5.91 pounds of trash a day. About 1.51 pounds of that gets recycled, which leaves 4.40 pounds on average per person as pure waste. Since cities do not have the resources to recycle all waste themselves, up until recently, the US was shipping its waste to Asia. In 2019, China banned the import of plastic and paper waste from other countries. Malaysia, Thailand, and India are all now stipulating stringent conditions and restrictions, citing environmental and public health concerns.

In the US, there is no national recycling program, and each city, county, and region manages their own waste reduction programs. These recycling programs can vary from exporting trash overseas, as mentioned above, to doing nothing at all, where collected household and commercial waste is sent to landfills. Even material that is shipped overseas for processing is seldom recycled since most of it is not deemed clean enough. It is often burned or taken to landfill. Pollutants eventually find their way into the environment. Each day, approximately eight million pieces of plastic pollution find their way into the world's rivers and oceans. There are around 5.25 trillion macro and micro plastic pieces floating in the open waters, weighing up to 269,000 tons.[30] The Pacific Garbage Patch is the largest of the five plastic and garbage accumulation zones in the world. Located halfway between Hawaii and California, it covers an approximate surface area of 1.6 million square kilometers, an area twice the size of Texas.

The company of the future will have to do business differently. The unrestricted use of natural resources, degradation of the natural environment, polluting of waterways, and the stripping of biodiversity, are no longer acceptable outcomes. Our planet is a closed-looped system: what goes around, comes around. The detrimental effects of our negative actions will have ripple effects for generations to come.

Case Study: Patagonia

An exemplary company focused on the **Preservation of the Future** is Patagonia. In September 2019, *TIME* magazine published an article, stating:

> "Patagonia has long been at the forefront of what is now emerging as an increasingly popular new flavor of capitalism. Today's customers want their dollars to go to companies that will use their money to make the world a better place. Patagonia donates 1 percent of sales to environmental nonprofits, and in 2016 gave 100 percent of Black Friday sales—about $10 million—to environmental groups. Late last year, it changed its mission statement to 'We're in business to save our home planet.' And on Sept 20, Patagonia shut down its stores and offices so that employees—including [CEO] Marcario—could strike alongside youth climate activists. 'Business has to pick up the mantle when the government fails you,' says Marcario, eating a bowl of hemp pesto pasta from the company's organic cafeteria. 'I think we've all realized that we have to go beyond 'Do no unnecessary harm,' a reference to part of the company's former motto... It was the first company to make fleece out of recycled bottles with its synthetic chinchilla, or 'synchilla,' which it unveiled in 1993. In 2005, it launched 'Worn Wear,' which sends employees to college campuses and climbing centers, teaching consumers how to repair things; the company also repairs customers' clothes in 72 repair centers globally."[31]

In studying Patagonia, a few things stand out:

1. Their commitment to go beyond 'doing no harm' to 'saving the planet' is a clear indication of Patagonia's understanding of the steward-leadership role it needs to play, given the realities of today.

2. Their conscious environmental activism to tap into belief-driven buyers, who choose a brand based on its position on social issues, is a sign of their unwavering commitment to building a meaningful relationship with their customers.

3. By teaching consumers how to sew and mend their clothes, they are acting as social change agents, to curb needless consumerism.

For the **Preservation of the Future** principle to be successfully implemented, the companies of tomorrow will similarly have to move from 'doing no harm' to 'saving the planet'. They will have to operate with a different paradigm, where the reward system will no longer be based on passing the buck to the younger generation. The sustainability of the business will be inextricably linked to the sustainability of the planet, including all its inhabitants. This integrative approach will require realigning vision with a powerful moral compass such as **MBI** to guide the company along the way. Not every company will survive this transformation, especially those that do not have a vision tied to a keen sense of right and wrong, and they will struggle in regaining the trust they have lost with many of their stakeholders.

According to the *2020 Edelman Trust Barometer* report, "... despite a strong global economy and near full employment, none of the four societal institutions that the study measures—government, business, NGOs and media—is trusted. The cause of this paradox can be found in people's fears about the future and their role in it, which are a wake-up call for our institutions to embrace a new way of effectively building trust: balancing competence with ethical behavior... A majority of respondents in every developed market do not believe they will be better off in five years' time, and more than half of respondents globally believe that capitalism in its current form is now doing more harm than good in the world".[32] The COVID-19 pandemic is hyper-accelerating these issues, adding fuel to a raging fire.

There is no magic wand that one can wave to close the trust gap. Building trust, to begin with, is a difficult task. Rebuilding it is going to be a long and uphill battle. A good start, however, is by providing consumers what they are looking for: eco-friendly and healthy options. Consumers are changing their behaviors and becoming conscious about the environment. Millennials on average are more risk-averse and less likely to spend money unnecessarily than previous generations. But when millennials do decide to part with their money, key patterns are beginning to emerge. They prefer to do business with corporations and brands with prosocial messages, sustainable manufacturing methods, and ethical business standards.

Businesses of tomorrow will be organizations that will contribute to society, and not simply extract from it. This will require transformation in the way business is conducted and the notion of what constitutes success. Leaders will have to acquire the courage, wisdom, and temperance to do the right thing against forces that will tell them otherwise. Board members will have to understand the relevance of **MBI** and how it relates to the responsibilities they shoulder. Lastly, senior executives will have to rethink, retrain, and retool to reframe the future leaders and workforce of their enterprise in alignment with the realities unfolding today, which are going to shape tomorrow.

Table 8 offers a simple maturity assessment guide to evaluate your organization's current role in the **Preservation of the Future**. It serves as a good starting point to quickly determine the critical success factors needed to implement this principle at your organization. As you go through the assessment, I would like you to keep the following questions in mind:

1. What are the accelerators and drivers for this principle at your organization?

2. Determine where your organization is on this chart. Then ask yourself: what are the inhibitors, challenges, and pitfalls that prevent advancement to the next stage?

Table 8: Preservation of the Future - Maturity Assessment

Stage 0 Subpar	Stage 1 Reactive	Stage 2 Developing	Stage 3 Advance	Stage 4 Leading
Preservation of the Future is not a critical component of business philosophy. No awareness of the environmental impact the organization is making. Succession planning is not included in the organizational structure.	The principle is invoked through the company's vision and mission statements that prescribes environmental and social rules, principles, values, and expectations. Follow through with inclusion in strategic planning is lacking.	Environmental protection, human health, and climate change are top strategic priorities. Decisions are occasionally based on impacts to the environment and future of the planet. The company is in process of, or has completed, an extensive materiality assessment to decipher sustainability-related priorities.	Support for sound environmental and social judgement is integrated in all decision making processes. Leaders are adept in leveraging Science Based Targets (SBTs), Life Cycle Analysis (LCAs), and other environmental and social impact assessment tools. Infusion of ESG issues into corporate culture, business strategy, and executive compensation plan is underway.	Leadership is actively engaged in continuously and holistically improving the supply-chains to rethink its role in society, and the impact their products and services have on the planet and the future generations. The company is publicly committed to resourcing substantial amounts of time, effort and money to fight many of the pressing environmental and social challenges we face today.

? Further Questions:

1 What do you need to do to adapt to these new environmental realities?

2 Are you putting the planet's well-being ahead of self-interest?

3 How well do you understand the social and environmental impact of the products and services you provide?

Chapter 10
Management by Intent:

> Yesterday I was clever, so I wanted to change the world. Today I am wise, so I am changing myself.
>
> — Jalāl ad-Dīn Rumi

IT IS THE character of the leadership that shapes the organization's value system, just like the tenacity and the intensity of the wind that shapes the dunes in the desert. But in spite of the sheer strength of the winds, the essence of the dunes remains the same: sand. In order to change the essence of sand, and transform the desert itself, water is needed. What water is to desert, intent is to character.

If a leader's character is grounded in an ethical and moral code of conduct, infused with a deep understanding of the **MBI Principles**, the end result leads to clarity of purpose, and outcomes that are tied to safeguarding the general public interest of all. I started this quest by helping my clients achieve meaningful results. It has culminated in the formulation of the **MBI Principles**. Over the course of my career, I have confronted the consequences of my actions, and forced myself to re-evaluate how genuinely aligned I was to living the principles outlined in this book.

As I evaluated and examined myself, by assessing my strategy and culture, I found that using the filters of **life**, **dignity**, **reason**, **wealth**, and the **future** helped me redress my path. It eventually led me to develop my consulting practice based on the **MBI Principles**. With this book, I aim to pay it forward.

When the **MBI Principles** are applied justly throughout the corporate decision-making process, they have the potential to become a driving force in refocusing an organization's mindset from short-term quarterly earnings into a broader and more balanced growth strategy; one dedicated to the cause of preventing harm and promoting good.

Over the course of my consulting career, I have met many exceptional leaders, yet few embody **MBI Principles** in its totality. I frequently get calls from senior executives who have been directed by their boards to find practical solutions to the ever-increasing onslaught of stakeholder demands; for a more robust plan of action regarding Environmental, Social and Governance (ESG) behavior.

As many CEOs jump on the sustainability bandwagon, hoping to find answers to pacify their shareholders, I give them this good-hearted advice: "Only focusing on tactical disclosure strategies is not going to cut it." That would be similar to simply slowing down your speed when you spot a cop. It is not just about obeying the law and not getting caught, but rather saving the lives of those in the car. Similarly, disclosing ESG policies and performance improvement statistics to pacify investors is not going to redress the root of the problem.

A vast percentage of the workforce, especially the younger generation, is growing wary of what our free enterprise system has evolved into. To rebalance the derailed free enterprise system, we need our leaders to be driven by a higher-level of consciousness; whereby they undertake sincere self-reflection to rebalance their own psyche, so that they attain the right wisdom, courage and temperance in dealing with some fundamental organizational and operational issues, redressing the rise in extreme inequity, resource scarcity, climate change, waste and pollution, destruction of ecosystems, and the loss of biodiversity.

I firmly believe that corporations can be a force of good for society. We already see many successful examples outlined throughout the chapters, such as Chobani and Patagonia.

There are signs of many other businesses wanting to start anew as well. At the 2020 World Economic Forum in Davos, the central theme echoing through the halls was the urgent need for business leaders to take up stakeholder capitalism. The need for companies to invest in their workers, while taking care of their customers, supporting their communities, and protecting the planet, has never been more pronounced.

MBI enables this agenda of change. It can be implemented by taking baby steps towards a future of principled inclusion that safeguards **life**, preserves **dignity**, upholds **reason**, protects **wealth**, and safeguards **future** generations.

Engendering a balance in capitalism will require recalibrating organizational intent. That goal requires a deep commitment to both behavioral, psychological, and structural level reformation. It necessitates profound transformational changes to the status quo business models, product portfolios, and practices across all enterprises. PepsiCo's PwP transformational initiative discussed in Chapter Two, took former CEO Nooyi and her team 10 years to implement. Such transformations are massive efforts designed to systematically realign the entire organization to its purpose. Even Wall Street is taking notice. It is no surprise that asset management firms such as BlackRock, a Wall Street powerhouse and holder of seven trillion dollars in global funds, is advancing an agenda of corporate sustainability and investment stewardship.

In January 2020, BlackRock Chairman and CEO Larry Fink disclosed the firm's perspective on prioritizing climate change as the defining factor for a business's long-term viability. Fink said that BlackRock is removing clients who earn more than 25% of their revenues from thermal coal production from its actively managed assets, citing overwhelming evidence of the direct impacts of climate change on both the physical world and the global system that finances economic growth. To that end, BlackRock set aside an ESG-focused portfolio. It based allocations on optimized sustainability factors and characteristics, instead of traditional market cap weightings. By the end of 2020, Fink promised to go public with that data.[33]

It is not just the investment community that is waking up to the stark reality of what lies ahead. Concerned leaders are now actively fighting the short-term earnings mentality. JUST Capital, a non-profit entity co-founded by a group of relevant business, finance, and civil society leaders, is an example of a focused effort to address the transformational shift needed to turn the tide towards a more equitable form of capitalism that serves all stakeholders.

As a mission-driven organization, JUST Capital's goal is to build an economy that works for all US citizens by helping companies improve how they serve their stakeholders. They believe that business and markets can and must be a greater force for good to address systemic issues such as income inequality and lack of opportunity. They tap into public priorities through their research, rankings, indexes, and data-driven tools to help measure and improve corporate performance in the stakeholder economy.

Another good example is the Alliance to End Plastic Waste, which is aggressively taking on the global challenge of decreasing the amount of plastic in the planet's oceans and waterways.

Complying with the UN Sustainable Development Goals, forming NGOs to redress global sustainability issues, or conforming to pressures from active or passive investors (such as shareholder proposals and their proxy statements) are all external forces that create change from the outside in.

However, infusing new life into legacy modus operandi will require strength of character and a demanding level of stick-to-itiveness, since cultures that feed on greed and excess will actively resist letting go of old habits to protect what they know best: their own interests. Hollow proclamations might help executives push to disclose sustainable performance improvements to their stakeholders, but mere disclosures would not be able to truly transform the culture, since it would be akin to pushing a boat into open waters, leaving it at the mercy of the waves.

Organizations that are just floating in the free enterprise capitalist ecosystem, without the intent of anchoring themselves to **MBI**-centric principles, will destroy what little public trust is left in the system.

It is already happening. According to the *2020 Edelman Trust Barometer* report, which surveyed 34,000 global respondents, capitalism is at an all-time low, with a 44% approval rating. The way Wall Street has behaved during the COVID-19 pandemic ensures that the ratings will take a further downward hit. Because, once again, the government's priority is Wall Street, not Main Street. Along with the airline industry, some 90,000 companies—amongst them private schools catering to an elite clientele, firms owned by foreign companies, and large chains backed by well-heeled Wall Street firms—got bailed out by the Paycheck Protection Program (PPP) funds, earmarked for small businesses. Many of these companies took the money without promising they would rehire workers or create jobs on their PPP loan applications.[34]

On July 18, 1914, J.H. Puelicher, then Vice President of Marshall & Ilsley Bank, was quoted in an article in the *Chicago Banker* articulating the effects of extravagance. He astutely asked the question: "Can we go on the way we are going?". He went on to say that history is replete with accounts of nations that rose while confronted with the hardships of development, but forgot that strong growth and rugged health were the results of vigorous efforts. They fell once they accomplished and reached the road to prosperity.[35]

It was not too long after that that the longest, most profound, and widespread depression of the 20th century enveloped the world, spinning economies out of control. The global GDP fell by 15%.

Wall Street's continued abject disregard of the consequences of its uncontrollable desire for money, coupled with the devastation reeked by

COVID-19, is hurtling us all towards a disaster. The time is ripe for active leadership engagement to begin the strategic transformation by looking deep within the organization to ascertain the delta to recalibrate the scales. Every CEO bears the responsibility to figure out what they need to do to change the current state of affairs, which has shaken people's trust to their very core. Captains of industry must redefine their organizational purpose to gain clarity of vision that accounts for the preservation of **life**, **dignity**, **reason**, **wealth**, and the **future**. Only then can purposeful sustainable growth be obtained.

Chobani, Patagonia, PepsiCo, and Organic Valley may be the frontrunners when it comes to embracing the essence of **MBI**, yet they are not alone. There is substantial evidence showing that many other companies have begun rethinking the purposefulness of the outcomes they are pursuing. Some have structured themselves as B Corporations which balance purpose and profit. At present, there are approximately 3,500 B Corporations around the world.

An increasing number of CEOs from traditional organizations are questioning the profit-only mentality. In August 2019, 181 Business Roundtable CEOs, including the leaders of JPMorgan Chase and Procter & Gamble, signed a letter committing to lead their companies for the benefit of customers, employees, suppliers, and communities, and not just shareholders. These are all hopeful and welcome signs of change.

I believe it is time for every CEO to step up and commit to an agenda for meaningful **MBI**-like change. The starting point for this commitment is internalizing the following **MBI** dictums:

- We are stewards of a closed-loop system called the Earth.

- Our responsibility to do good is directly proportional to the reach and impact of our products and services.

- Doing good requires the ability to reflect and reason, inducing harmony between our emotional, behavioral, and cognitive systems, and tying us to a higher level of consciousness.

- We must exhibit wisdom, courage, and temperance to get to our purposeful outcomes.

- We have to become systems thinkers to understand the structure and complexity of the whole, keeping in view the interrelationship and interdependence of its parts, before we act.

- Our actions must reflect the preservation of life, dignity, reason, wealth, and the future as universal principles to be part of our short-term and long-term strategic imperatives.

- To be holistically and wholly successful, we need to partner and collaborate with all stakeholders.

I started the book asking the following five questions:

1. What does **MBI** look like?

2. Would **MBI** be feasible and practical to deploy?

3. Would **MBI** offer a more holistic transformational mechanism for creating balance in society?

4. Would **MBI** have a positive impact on the current financial centric ways of assessing organizational performance?

5. Is **MBI** a catalyst for holistic positive change?

A simple answer to all these questions is: yes, it can! It is my belief that **MBI Principles** can lead to radical purpose-oriented transformation. The goal is to understand when to pivot off the decades-old playbook and how to embrace the new game plan. For many, the COVID-19 pandemic will be the trigger event. Since every organization is different, the **MBI** roadmap will be custom-made to suit the capacity and sophistication of the organization. The **Maturity Diagnostic Tables** in Chapters Five through Nine are a good first step in the right direction.

In the *Divine Governance of the Human Kingdom*, Ibn 'Arabi, an Andalusian scholar, mystic, poet, and philosopher of the 12th century, aptly stated:

> ...now that you know the reality of the people of your realm, give them the different things that they need, while not forgetting your own needs: to some, knowledge, to some, wisdom, to some, what they lack in perfection; to some, help with your actions. To all show generosity, without surpassing its boundaries.[36]

This book is a call to action for leaders to initiate positive change by using **MBI** principles. **MBI** assists businesses, whether they are for-profit, non-profit, conglomerates, small, global or regional.

I urge you to take a deep look at your organization through the **MBI** lens. As parting words, I leave you with the following poem:

The Abyss
by Abrar Ansari

We stand at the cliff, edging towards the abyss
Destroying our way of life, searching for bliss
Startled by our inability to comprehend
Unable to see the damage and to amend
Intoxicated with extravagance, programmed to consume
Devouring the planet, to our inevitable doom
Pillaging, ravaging, polluting our home
Unreflective of the root cause of all we bemoan
Clinging to a rhetoric steeped in greed
We are poised to destroy the human creed
Living in a state of heedlessness it seems
Where equity and justice are no longer the dreams
Locked up we are in demented realities
The shareholders are all we are trying to appease
Aren't we supposed to be dignified and elevated?
Stewards of this planet, mindful and calculated?
Our leaders enrich themselves at the expense of the public
Our free enterprise system a farce, a banana republic
Misguided are our loyalties, our sense of ethics a joke
Our corporation amass wealth, on the backs of working-class folk
What oxygen is to our blood, introspection is to our thought
When our intellect is without reasoning, our character starts to rot
What we do today has far-reaching repercussions
The time has long gone, to sit and have discussions

Organizational Psyche

Emotional
Behavioral
Cognitive

	Typical Organization Psyche and Resulting Behavior	MBI Organization Psyche and Resulting Behavior
Intent	Excessive / Deficient	Balanced
Action	Self-preservation	Preservation of Life, Dignity, Reason, Wealth & Future
Purposeful Outcomes	Short-term financial gains 1. Preserving shareholders wealth 2. Promoting revenue & profitability	Long-term public interest 1. Preventing that which is harmful 2. Promoting that which is good

MBI Deployment Framework

ESTABLISH
the **business** case for integrating the 5 principles

CONDUCT
an **MBI maturity assessment** to identify delta between "current state" and future state

IDENTIFY
the right **metrics** to track your progress towards desired MBI maturity level (i.e. outcomes)

DEVELOP
an **MBI roadmap** and identify initiatives that can be leveraged to reach the desired outcomes

REFINE/BUILD
the support **systems** necessary to achieve your plans

INITIATE
the MBI transformation

Notes

Chapter 2

1. Indra K. Nooyi and Vijay Govindarajan, "Becoming a Better Corporate Citizen," *Harvard Business Review*, March–April, 2020, accessed September 9, 2020, https://hbr.org/2020/03/becoming-a-better-corporate-citizen.

2. "Our Humble History", About Us, Organic Valley, accessed November 16, 2019, www.organicvalley.coop/about-us/our-humble-history.

Chapter 3

3. Imam Muhammad Al-Ghazzali, *Alchemy of Happiness*, trans. Jay R. Crook (Chicago: Kazi Publications, 2005).

4. Gary Rivlin, "A Giant Pile of Money," The Intercept, October 20, 2018, accessed September 9, 2020, https://theintercept.com/2018/10/20/public-pensions-crisis-wall-street-fees.

5. Bethany Barnes, "Moving Millions, Leaving Mayhem," *Tampa Bay Times*, March 1, 2020, accessed September 9, 2020, https://projects.tampabay.com/projects/2020/investigations/garda-world/armored-trucks.

Chapter 5

6. "National Census of Fatal Occupational Injuries in 2018," News Release, Bureau of Labor Statistics, US Department of Labor, December 17, 2019, accessed December 15, 2020, https://www.bls.gov/news.release/pdf/cfoi.pdf.

7. "Commonly Used Statistics," Occupational Safety and Health Administration, United States Department of Labor, 2018, accessed December 15, 2020, https://www.osha.gov/data/commonstats.

8. "Workplace Stress," Info, The American Institute of Stress, accessed January 8, 2020, https://www.stress.org/workplace-stress.

9. "Human rights and the protection of workers from exposure to toxic substances," SR Hazardous Substances and Waste, Environment, Office of the High Commissioner for Human Rights, accessed January 17, 2020, https://www.ohchr.org/EN/Issues/Environment/ToxicWastes/Pages/RightsWorkersToxicChemicalExposure.aspx.

10. Cora Peterson, Aaron Sussell, Jia Li, Pamela K. Schumacher, Kristin Yeoman and Deborah M. Stone, "Suicide Rates by Industry and Occupation — National Violent Death Reporting System, 32 States, 2016," *Morbidity and Mortality Weekly Report,* Centers for Disease Control and Prevention, 2020; 69(3):57–62, accessed September 9, 2020, https://www.cdc.gov/mmwr/volumes/69/wr/mm6903a1.htm.

11. Evan W. Carr, Andrew Reece, Gabriella Rosen Kellerman and Alexi Robichaux, "The Value of Belonging at Work," *Harvard Business Review,* December 16, 2019, accessed September 9, 2020, https://hbr.org/2019/12/the-value-of-belonging-at-work.

Chapter 6

12. Mark W. Bennett, Justin D. Levinson and Koichi Hioki, "Judging Federal White-Collar Fraud Sentencing: An Empirical Study Revealing the Need for Further Reform," *Iowa Law Review*, 2017; 102(3), accessed March 5, 2020, https://ilr.law.uiowa.edu/print/volume-102-issue-3/judging-federal-white-collar-fraud-sentencing-an-empirical-study-revealing-the-need-for-further-reform.

13. Michael Winston, "Why have no CEOs been punished for the financial crisis?," *The Hill*, December 8, 2016, accessed September 9, 2020, https://thehill.com/blogs/pundits-blog/finance/309544-why-have-no-ceos-been-punished-for-the-financial-crisis.

14. Kaushik Viswanath, "Companies Don't Need to Lay People Off to Survive," *Marker–Medium*, April 9, 2020, accessed September 9, 2020, https://marker.medium.com/companies-dont-need-to-lay-people-off-to-survive-4197a9e57f6c.

15. Winnie Byanyima, "Supermarket supply chains are driving poverty and inequality. We can do better," Agenda, World Economic Forum, June 25, 2018, accessed September 9, 2020, https://www.weforum.org/agenda/2018/06/supermarket-supply-chains-driving-poverty-inequality-winnie-byanyima-oxfam.

16. "Workplace Dignity Survey," Insights, Willis Towers Watson, February 5, 2020, accessed September 9, 2020, https://www.willistowerswatson.com/en-US/Insights/2020/01/2019-workplace-dignity-survey.

17. Anna Powers, "A Study Finds That Diverse Companies Produce 19% More Revenue," *Forbes*, June 27, 2018, accessed September 9, 2020, https://www.forbes.com/sites/annapowers/2018/06/27/a-study-finds-that-diverse-companies-produce-19-more-revenue/#914dec4506f3.

18. Marcel Schwantes, "The CEO of Salesforce Found Out His Female Employees Were Paid Less Than Men. His Response is Priceless," *Inc.*, accessed April 12, 2020, https://www.inc.com/marcel-schwantes/the-ceo-of-salesforce-found-out-female-employees-are-paid-less-than-men-his-response-is-a-priceless-leadership-lesson.html.

Chapter 7

19. "Volkswagen with New Corporate Mission Statement Environment 'goTOzero'," News, Volkswagen, July 10, 2019, accessed April 12, 2020, https://www.volkswagenag.com/en/news/2019/07/goTOzero.html.

Chapter 8

20. "ALICE Essentials Index," *2020 National Report*, United for ALICE, May 2020, accessed September 9, 2020, https://www.unitedforalice.org/essentials-index.

21. Chris Isidore, "Gravity Payments CEO takes 90% pay cut to give workers huge raise," CNN Business, April 15, 2015, accessed September 9, 2020, https://money.cnn.com/2015/04/14/news/companies/ceo-pay-cuts-pay-increases/index.html.

22. Erik Sherman, "A New Report Claims Big Tech Companies Used Legal Loopholes to Avoid Over $100 Billion in Taxes. What does that mean for the Industry's Future?," Fortune, December 6, 2019, accessed September 9, 2020, https://fortune.com/2019/12/06/big-tech-taxes-google-facebook-amazon-apple-netflix-microsoft.
23. "Fact Sheet: Offshore Corporate Loopholes," Americans for Tax Fairness, accessed March 15, 2020, https://americansfortaxfairness.org/tax-fairness-briefing-booklet/fact-sheet-offshore-corporate-tax-loopholes.
24. Tam Harbert, "Here's how much of the 2008 bailouts really cost," MIT Sloan Management School, February 21, 2019, accessed September 9, 2020, https://mitsloan.mit.edu/ideas-made-to-matter/heres-how-much-2008-bailouts-really-cost.
25. Stephanie Strom, "At Chobani, Now It's Not Just the Yogurt That's Rich," *The New York Times*, April 26, 2016, accessed September 9, 2020, https://www.nytimes.com/2016/04/27/business/a-windfall-for-chobani-employees-stakes-in-the-company.html.

Chapter 9

26. "Executive Summary," *Global Risks Report 2020,* World Economic Forum, January 15, 2020, accessed September 9, 2020, http://www3.weforum.org/docs/WEF_Global_Risk_Report_2020.pdf.
27. Nick Paton Walsh and Vasco Cotovio, "Bats are not to blame for coronavirus. Humans are," Health, CNN, March 20, 2020, accessed September 9, 2020, https://edition.cnn.com/2020/03/19/health/coronavirus-human-actions-intl/index.html.
28. Frederica Perera, "The Womb is No Protection From Toxic Chemicals," *the New York Times,* July 1, 2017, accessed September 9, 2020, https://www.nytimes.com/2017/06/01/opinion/toxic-chemicals-pregnancy-fetus.html.
29. World Health Organization, 2009 GLOBAL HEALTH RISKS; Mortality and burden of disease attributable to selected major risks, accessed September 9, 2020, https://www.who.int/healthinfo/global_burden_disease/GlobalHealthRisks_report_full.pdf
30. "Plastic Pollution-Facts and Figures,", Surfers Against Sewage, accessed April 16, 2020, https://www.sas.org.uk/our-work/plastic-pollution/plastic-pollution-facts-figures.
31. Alana Semuels, "'Rampant Consumerism Is Not Attractive.' Patagonia Is Climbing to the Top — and Reimagining Capitalism Along the Way," *TIME*, September 23, 2019, accessed September 9, 2020, https://time.com/5684011/patagonia.
32. Edelman Intelligence, *2020 Edelman Trust Barometer*, January 19, 2020, accessed September 9, 2020, https://www.edelman.com/trustbarometer

Chapter 10

33. Larry Fink, "A Fundamental Reshaping of Finance," BlackRock, accessed April 20, 2020, https://www.blackrock.com/corporate/investor-relations/larry-fink-ceo-letter.

34. Jonathan O'Connell, Aaron Gregg, Steven Rich, Anu Narayanswamy and Peter Whoriskey, Treasury, "SBA data show small-business loans went to private-equity backed chains, members of Congress," *The Washington Post*, June 6, 2020, accessed September 9, 2020, https://www.washingtonpost.com/business/2020/07/06/sba-ppp-loans-data.

35. J.H. Puelicher, *the Chicago Banker,* July 18, 1914, accessed April 23, 2020, J. H. Puelicher Makes Thrift Talk at Milwaukee Convention,

36. Ibn 'Arabi, *Divine Governance of the Human Kingdom*, trans. Tosun Bayrak Al Jerrahi Al Halvet (Louisville: Fons Vitae, 1997).

www.ingramcontent.com/pod-product-compliance
Lightning Source LLC
Chambersburg PA
CBHW051857160426
43209CB00039B/1972/J